130775

9.95

7.95

6.95

5.95

4.95

2.95

Win
With
BOB
AVILA

By Juli S. Thorson

Published by
Western Horseman Inc.
3850 North Nevada Ave.
Box 7980
Colorado Springs, CO 80933-7980

Design, Typography, and Production
Darin Edmonds, Western Horseman
Colorado Springs, Colorado

Photography by
Jim Bortvedt
Portland, Oregon

Printing
Publisher's Press
Salt Lake City, Utah

First Printing: September 2000

ISBN 0-911647-57-0

DEDICATION

I'D LIKE to dedicate this book to the two people who've influenced me the most in my career and my life in general. Though my name's in the book's title, there's probably more of their knowledge and teachings in each chapter than there is of mine.

The first person is my father, Don Avila. Like most kids, I didn't fully appreciate all my father taught me until I became much older. Now I feel very lucky to have had such a great horseman for a father, and luckier yet to have this chance to say so.

The second person is Tony Amaral, the late California trainer and horseman who was my idol from the time I was a little boy until he died in 1998. Tony didn't just take me on as an apprentice some 30 years ago. He also helped me grow up and inspired me to settle for nothing less than excellence in all I try to do.

Dad, Tony—this book exists because of you.

—Bob Avila

Tony Amaral (left) and Don Avila.

DEDICATION & ACKNOWLEDGEMENT

I DEDICATE my work on *Win With Bob Avila* to the memory of my late grandfather, Francis J. Smith. Horse lover and horseman extraordinaire, he took pleasure in sharing first-hand knowledge that could help others reach their own goals with horses. The horse industry went through many evolutions in his lifetime (1905-1980), yet he didn't look back—he looked forward. He jumped on change and took advantage of it, before it took advantage of him. He knew how to think to win, and would tell you how to do it if you were open-minded enough to listen to him. As my earliest horse mentor, Grandpa Smith left an indelible impression, and would have been first in line to buy this book.

I also wish to express gratitude to the many editors and publishers who, over the years, have entrusted me with their most valuable resource—their readers, students, and customers. A heartfelt "thanks for the break you gave me" to: Don Witham, publisher, *West Fargo Pioneer*; Don Walker, editor, *Appaloosa News*; George B. Hatley, executive secretary, Appaloosa Horse Club Inc.; Ivar Nelson and Patricia Hart, owners and publishers, North Country Book Express; Don Coombs, chairman, School of Communications, University of Idaho; Barbara Zellner, publisher, *The Lariat* and *In Stride*; Jennifer Forsberg Meyer, publisher, *California Horse Review*; Pamela Goold, publisher, *Performance Horseman;* Harry Myers, publisher, *Horse & Rider*; Tom Winsor, publisher, *Ride With Bob Avila*; and most recently, the horsemen and -women whom I've been privileged to join at *Western Horseman*.

Finally, I'll seize this chance to acknowledge the horseman, collaborator, and friend who's been the greatest mentoring force for me of them all—Bob Avila. Not a day goes by that I don't benefit in some way from the knowledge and advice he shares so openly.

—*Juli S. Thorson*

Why do some goal-seeking horse people manage to become champions, while others never pass a certain plateau?

Why is one owner or breeder able to sell more horses, for more money, than his neighbor?

Why will one performance-bred yearling sell for $100,000 at auction, while another by the same sire gets no buyer interest at a tenth of the other's price?

How much more successful might you become in your pursuit of horse-world success if you just could get the chance to be taken under the wing of a top-notch professional horseman?

You'll find answers to these and other questions in *Win With Bob Avila*. It's an insight tool designed to take you beyond the subject of how a winner trains his horses and into the breakthrough zone of what makes a winner, inside and outside the show pen, in today's western performance-horse industry.

As I've had the opportunity to do since 1983, you'll join Bob Avila at his everyday workday world, a hilltop horse facility in the eastward shadow of Oregon's Coast Range mountains. You'll watch him ride a day's worth of world-caliber horses, and be on hand as he works with his customers, assistant trainers, barn helpers, vet and farrier, and others. You'll also accompany Bob to nearby Bryant Ranch, the breeding farm that stands a battery of his retired performance champions.

While you're making this unique visual visit, you'll have access, as Bob's regular associates do, to his unique brand of success-driven thinking. He'll give you his advice, tips, analysis, and opinions on topics ranging from trends in the breeding, buying, and selling of western-breed horses to the benefits to be had from going that "little extra" in key areas of your horse program.

Ultimately, you'll learn that there's more, way more, to becoming successful than knowing how to ride and train horses. Whether you seek to sharpen your edge as a success-seeking exhibitor, breeder, owner, or trainer, you can think of *Win With Bob Avila* as your mentor in print.

By anyone's measure, Bob is qualified to coach others about how to improve their horse programs and reach their goals. Since

childhood, when he was a winning junior rider at West Coast shows, he's mixed hands-on experience with ahead-of-the-curve perspective to become one of the most versatile and successful professional horsemen you could name.

Bob's won American Quarter Horse Association world championships in cutting, reining, working cow horse, western riding, and halter. He's earned a Superhorse title, awarded to the high-point all-around horse at the AQHA World Show, and has campaigned numerous AQHA year-end national high-point champions since his first one in 1975.

Bob's also the only competitor (as of 1999) to win both the National Reining Horse Association and National Reined Cow Horse Association futurities, and their first-place checks for $100,000. In 1995 his peers voted him AQHA Professional Horseman of the Year, making him the first person to receive the honor. In 2000 he capped his competitive career thus far by winning the World's Greatest Horseman title in a grueling all-around contest.

And that's just for starters. Due to the similarly impressive accomplishments of professionals who've served apprenticeships under him, Bob's earned a reputation as "the trainer's trainer."

Besides that, Bob's guided many youths and non-pros to reach goals of their own, in the show ring and out. For example, some of his customers have become successful breeders, while others have applied his principles to reach their goals in different horse-related businesses. Bob's also been a trend-setter in equine marketing, stallion promotion, seminars and clinics, videos and publications, and endorsements.

In short, when it comes to guiding others onto the insider track for achieving success in the western performance-horse world,

Bob is someone who can walk the talk.

He places great importance in establishing and maintaining this brand of been-there-done-that credibility.

"It's a personal thing with me," he says. "I strive to be successful as a way of proving that my ideas and observations are ones that work. I don't want to be the kind of adviser who tells you how to do something but can't actually do it himself. I'd also rather get right to the meat of a matter than waste your time by handing out candy."

To that end, Bob doesn't sugar-coat his advice and opinions in the effort to make you feel good. When you ask for his feedback, he says exactly what he thinks and why, in a way that has a tendency to be swiftly enlightening.

He does this with what might be called a whole-brain approach. Bob's a supreme realist with X-ray vision to the factual core of any problem—just what your left brain craves. But he's also able to get through to your right brain by using analogies and comparisons that paint images of understanding.

Those qualities rarely occur in the same person, and when they do, you've found an effective communicator—this time, one who's not afraid to put spurs to some of your preset beliefs.

With noted exceptions, the photographs for this book were taken by Jim Bortvedt.

Jim was familiar with the turf. He's been meeting me at Avila Stables to photograph instructional material for horse people since the early 1980s.

I think you'll enjoy Jim's you-are-there eye. He comes by it well after spending over 30 years as a show, ranch, and publications photographer. Like Bob, he can translate explanation into imagery. And like Bob, he's got great feel and timing, and an appreciation for each horse as an individual. I've never had to tell Jim what details a horse person would want to see in in a photograph. He already knows.

It's my hope that the material in this book will help you to pursue your horse goals, whatever they are, with freshened perspective, renewed motivation, and a champion's commitment to excellence.

That's how I always feel after a visit to Bob's domain, and now you get to go there too.

—Juli S. Thorson

Win With BOB AVILA

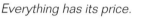

CONTENTS

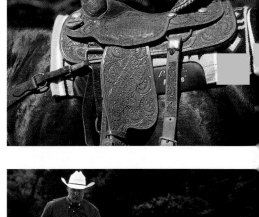

With the Mindset You Choose

YOU DON'T have to be a show rider to be someone who wants to win with horses. To me, winning is synonymous with reaching goals—with getting where you set out to go—and that brand of winning means different things to different people.

To one person, winning might mean being the breeder of an outstanding horse. His neighbor might define it as having trained, shown, and sold a world champion. Someone else might feel like a winner for finally having found his dream horse after a string of disappointing buys, or for overcoming a chronic problem in a horse.

Your version of reaching a goal could be anywhere in between. It just depends on where your horse-related interest lies, and how high you want to set your sights within that area.

Of course, just because you have a personal vision of success doesn't necessarily mean it'll materialize. The horse world is occupied by a good number of people who never manage to reach their goals despite the best of intentions.

So what sets the achievers apart?

I've come in contact with many successful horsemen and -women at all levels of the horse industry, pro and non-pro, and have learned they have traits in common. Unsuccessful horse people have traits in common, too, except theirs is a different set.

There's an old saying ...
You make your own luck.

I'm a firm believer that every one of us has the choice of which set of traits to use as we try to achieve something with horses. And that choice, if you ask me, is the first thing that separates winners from losers, the successful from the unsuccessful, and the achievers from the also-rans.

When it comes to horsemanship knowledge and ability, everyone starts out equally, at zero. How far you go from there is entirely up to you. Winning is what you make of it.

Goal-Advancing Traits

Ask yourself: How many of these traits do I possess, and which ones am I missing?

The horse world is plagued by the persistent belief that money determines who succeeds and who doesn't. Nothing could be farther from the truth. Attitude is what makes the difference. It doesn't matter whether you're a 4-H member struggling to get out of the white-ribbon group or an experienced competitor chasing after a world title; your outlook controls your outcome.

The people who reach their goals in the horse world, at any level, are usually open-minded. They don't fight change. Instead, they find a way to harness it. Successful horse people are willing to acknowledge when they've made a mistake. They learn from it and go on instead of making excuses.

When they reach a "stuck" place and need help, those who become successful ask for it and are discriminating about who they turn to. They take free advice for what it's worth. When they've paid good money to get assistance, they're willing to change in the direction their adviser recommends.

The majority of goal-reaching horse people are analytical thinkers who operate more off reason than emotion. They discipline themselves to take a problem apart in their minds, so they can pinpoint the why of the problem as a starting place for solving it.

They've also honed the ability to break a long-term goal down into a series of smaller goals that they tackle one at a time. They don't procrastinate, but think in terms of

"what can I do today to get even the tiniest bit better?"

When goal-achieving horse people have a bad year or season, or any other kind of setback, they don't waste energy on finding someone or something to blame. They figure out what they need to be doing differently, then dig in and go back to work. What others consider unfair politics, they see as the realities of human nature. They also seek knowledge constantly and keep up with trends.

The horse people in the winners group choose their company and their mentors wisely. They steer clear of negative people, and model themselves after individuals who've already become successful in their area of interest. Instead of resenting the success of others, they try to learn from it.

They also build a strong network of allies and contacts, ranging from their farrier and veterinarian to friends who can be counted on in an emergency. They acknowledge the

The most successful horse people make a conscious effort to model themselves after people who're already at the level they aspire to. They seek advice from qualified sources and act on the counsel they're given.

Some people believe motivation breeds action. I think it's the other way around. All the motivation in the world won't do anything for your goal if you don't take take deliberate action to move in your chosen direction.

success

SUCCESS LESSON

I don't want anyone to think I've always been Mr. Goody Two-Shoes, because I haven't. I did some really stupid things in public before I learned how to control my temper. Someone who reads this book is going to say, 'I can remember when Bob Avila buried a ribbon in the arena.' And I did do that, at a Quarter Horse show in the 1970s. I made a run that I thought was fabulous, but the judge gave me third or fourth. I dropped my ribbon in the dirt right in front of him and buried it like a dog would do, just to show that judge what I thought. Afterward, I got a letter from AQHA that said, in effect, "If you ever do anything like that again, you'll never get to play our game again." That shaped me up real quick. I came close to ruining my career before it had barely started.

power of presentation, and take the best possible care of their horses. They have a plan for everything, and work their plan.

And, believing that "what goes around comes around," the most successful horse people tend to be those who willingly give back to the horse industry in some way. They share their time, talent, and ideas, and would rather help find solutions to problems than sit back and complain about them.

Goal-Limiting Traits

Ask yourself: *Which of these traits have I been using, and how have they held me back?*

In contrast with those who attain success, the horse people who don't end up reaching goals tend to be stuck in their ways. They're stubborn, won't admit when they're wrong, and won't listen to other people. They can be hot-headed, with misdirected motivation. They usually allow their emotions to rule most of their decisions and actions.

Unsuccessful horse people are resistant to change. They tend to be more concerned about "the good old days" than about accepting and learning from what's new. They're negative instead of positive, and seem to enjoy being in the company of other negative people who'll join them in their griping.

They're also selfish. Their attitude toward giving back to the horse industry is one of "let the other guy do it."

The unsuccessful often suffer from bad cases of what my late friend and adviser Ben Scott used to call "I'll Show 'Em Disease," meaning that they're more interested in proving a point than in improving themselves and their horses.

For instance, they'll refuse to update their bloodlines, saying, "If judges think that's what it takes to win these days, I'll prove them wrong." They insist on trying to buck

The sooner you identify and learn to control your most vulnerable emotion (a bad temper is mine), the more successful you'll be in any aspect of the horse world. We all have an inner enemy that'll beat us if we let it.

When you can look past color to spot physical ability, you'll have the start of a professional's eye for horses.

the system, and want to be the exception to its rules. "Yeah, but ..." is one of their favorite phrases.

I don't know if people are born with a tendency toward one set of traits or not. But I do know it's possible to change something about yourself once you admit that you'll be holding yourself back if you don't.

I'm proof of that. For the sake of helping you take a critical look at your own goal-limiting traits, I'm willing to confess I have a bad temper that got me into trouble earlier in my career. I've had to teach myself to keep a grip on this destructive emotion because I know from experience what happens when I don't.

Another Decision

Ask yourself: Is my approach to my goal going to be personal or professional?

The choice you make here will affect almost every area of your goal pursuit, because it'll influence your subsequent decisions and the results you'll get. In general, the closer you come to the professional approach, the more readily you'll attain your goal.

The path you choose will be based on more criteria than whether you qualify for a non-pro card or declare your horse activities as a business to the Internal Revenue Service. I've met card-holding non-pros who manage their horse ventures more professionally than some

trainers do, and also know plenty of people who say their horses are a business, but act otherwise.

The best way for me to clarify the difference between the personal and professional approaches is to give you some examples taken from my experience as an adviser to other horse people.

Let's say you've asked me to find you a talented reining prospect that you can have started and then resell at a profit. You give me an ample budget but also insist, for whatever reason, that the horse be a palomino.

My response is going to be in the form of a question: What does palomino coloring have to do with whether a horse is a talented reining prospect? Nothing.

A professional-minded horse buyer wouldn't impose this kind of personal-preference limitation on his field of choices. He'd insist on

STRAIGHT TRUTH

You can't force the public to buy what it doesn't want. If purple horses are in demand and you insist on breeding orange ones because you like those better, you might end up with a pasture full of beautiful orange horses. But that doesn't mean you can expect to be as successful as the breeders of purple horses.

talent first, then accept whatever color it came in. He'd say, "This horse isn't exactly what I had in mind, but he's a good horse, so I'll go with him."

Next, imagine that you've raised a cutting-bred colt that you're proud of. You decide to take him to a top trainer to be started and evaluated as a potential cutter. He calls you after the first 30 or 60 days and tells you that in his professional opinion, the horse lacks ability in the field you've chosen for him.

He recommends that you sell the colt, at a loss if necessary, before putting any more money into him. What do you do?

If you're professional in your approach, you'll take the advice you've just paid good money to get. You'll deal no differently with this setback to your goal than you would when hearing your accountant say, "Sorry to have to tell you this, but you're going to owe more tax this year." Yes, it's a bummer, but

you'll "cowboy up" and move on.

If you're personal in your approach, you'll choose to do otherwise. For example, instead of selling, you may send the horse to a succession of other trainers with hopes of a different outcome.

Maybe this is a horse you love, and you'll do anything to give him the chance you feel he deserves. Maybe you care more about proving your horse's worth than you do about ever making a dime on him. Maybe you keep going with this horse because you can't bring yourself to sell him. Maybe you want to spare the feelings of a family member who would be upset if you sold the horse.

Those are perfectly fine objectives, from a personal point of view. Where people get into trouble in pursuit of goals is when they want their horses to serve their personal needs, but want them to be winners and/or moneymakers as well. The sets of objectives don't mesh most of the time.

There's no question that the horse industry feeds off personal preference and recreational

When a horse has come this far in my training program, he's passed a lot of tests. I won't keep taking a customer's money to continue training a horse who lacks physical and mental ability to perform at a high level.

imagery

MIND PICTURE

Become a mirror of the horse people you look up to. By reflecting them in attitude and action, you'll bring your own success picture into clearer view.

spending. But if you're going to be in the industry for profit, or as a trainer, breeder, or competitor who wants to reach the top of a level or discipline, you have to get rid of some of your preferences in favor of what the marketplace wants. The higher you want to go, the more this is true.

That's part of taking the professional approach. Instead of fighting them, you learn to go along with changes, trends, and adviser tips, and to employ objectivity in all you do.

With the professional approach, you won't just be tuned into current trends. You'll also be motivated to spend your money wisely, just as a prudent businessman or -woman would do in order to survive and thrive. The personal approach doesn't impose that discipline, and as a result, you can end up making decisions that bump you off the road to your goal.

I see this happen all time. Operating from the personal approach, some people will spend more on their show clothing than they do on their horse care, or more on short-lived faddish tack than they do on quality gear that lasts. They'll overextend themselves financially just so they can drive a truck and trailer as nice as their neighbor's.

The next thing you know, they're cutting corners on essentials like feed and farrier care, or breeding their mares to cheaper stallions. As the value of their stock declines, they'll complain loudly that "the average person can't

make it in the horse industry." Yet the structure of the horse industry isn't to blame for what are self-inflicted problems.

I'm not saying you can't treat your horses as a hobby or have fun with your horses, or that you have to be completely without feeling in order to be successful. To be a good horseman of any kind, I think you have to love your animals and treat them as valued individuals. I also believe that few people reach a goal, whatever their approach, without having a passion for their pursuit.

What I am saying is that you'll be most successful by matching your expectations to the approach you take. If you're most comfortable with the personal approach, and don't mind that it'll probably cost more and take longer to reach your goal than if you'd chosen the professional approach, that's great.

Just realize you've made a conscious choice to go in this direction. If you do reach your goal without a struggle, or end up making a little money off your horse hobby, regard either result as a bonus, not something that's guaranteed.

objectivity

Tools for Making Choices

When you're involved with horses, you face many occasions of having to choose between one course of action or another. Use this set of professional-approach questions as a tool for getting past the crossroads.

- What's the biggest horse-related decision I face at present?

- What are the choices of action?

- What consequences, negative and positive, do I foresee from each choice?

- What variables of each choice's consequences are out of my control?

- What variables are under my control?

- What's the worst thing that could happen as a result of my making any of the choices?

- If the worst thing did happen, could I live with it?

- What's the best thing that could happen as a result of my making any of the choices?

- If the best thing did occur, how would it advance me toward my goal?

- Based on my previous answers, which choice stands the best chance of helping me get where I want to go?

by Rising to Meet
Your Challenge

I'M GOING to come right out and say it: Anything you want to achieve with horses is going to take discipline and hard work. It's the kind of work no one else can do for you, because it's much more mental than physical. If dreams and talent were enough, everyone would be a world champion, a renowned breeder, or other kind of star.

I think we've all known people who talk big about having horse goals, and yet always have an excuse for not going forward. They put more energy into coming up with justifications than they do in sticking to the concept of "just do it."

That's a big reason why such people are seldom successful past a certain point. Their true motivation isn't to succeed, it's to avoid failure by playing it safe. They back down to their comfort zone the minute the going gets tough.

To me, that's the ultimate self-sabotage, because the going always gets tough at some point when you're dealing with horses and human emotions. Illness, injury, lack of money, stiffer competition, family problems, depleted confidence—name a setback, and chances are you'll come up against it sometime. There's a lot of truth to the phrase, "No guts, no glory."

Even though dreamers may outnumber doers by at least 10 to 1, the horse world still has no shortage of individuals who are driven and determined. Perhaps because I'm known

There's an old saying ...
Everything has its price.

to have those same traits, I seem to come in contact with a good share of such folks. Declaring that they're willing to make any sacrifice, they often ask me what it really takes to reach the top in certain areas of the horse industry, so they'll know what to expect.

Typical questions: "How do I become a champion?" "What's the best way to get started as a trainer?" "What are the secrets to raising great horses?" "How do I 'make it' as a stallion owner?"

You'll find my answers on the following pages.

"Always do the hardest thing first"
is a principle I live by. I apply it to
everything, from the discipline of
riding daily, to my belief that appren-
tices should learn the training busi-
ness from the ground up.

success

SUCCESS LESSON

I've always remembered something my dad drilled into me about the horse business when I was just a kid: You make it or break it on horse care. You can't guarantee that an owner's mare will get in foal or that his horse will win. But if the horse leaves your place shiny, bathed, and clipped, the owner won't find disappointment so tough to take. At least he'll drive off with pride in his horse intact.

One of my assistants, Trent Pederson.

Becoming a Champion

Key to success: You can't deny or ignore your weaknesses. You need to identify them and then strategize ways to strengthen them.

At every level of every discipline, a select few competitors become known as the ones to beat. Call them the top guns, the big boys, the stars, whatever you will; they're the rulers of their games.

Are they the ones with the most push-button horses? No. They're the ones who work the hardest and smartest. Granted, you must have a good horse to become a champion, but that's only half the picture. Even the greatest horse doesn't show himself.

I find that many competitors have never really sat down and considered just exactly what skills they need in order to win at their game. Some remain especially unaware of how their emotions and behaviors affect them. That's a limitation, because you can't work to improve something when you aren't aware that it's a factor.

Naturally, you need certain physical skills in order to show a horse, and you probably could name your weakest ones. Maybe you have trouble with transitions, for example, or haven't yet mastered lead changes. Those definitely need to be on your "Needs Work" list.

But beyond the physical, where else could you have weaknesses that need your attention? Here's a partial list of possibilities to get you started thinking in that direction.

• Time management. Do you always do everything at the last minute? Do you find yourself rushing to get ready for classes? Do you spend most of your warm-up time gabbing with other riders instead of learning your course or pattern?

• Organization. Do you often have to borrow gear because you've forgotten items of yours at home? Do you sometimes arrive at shows without your checkbook, registration papers, and membership cards? Would you "forget your head if it wasn't screwed on"?

• Emotions management. Do you lose your cool when something goes wrong right before a class? Are you easily intimidated by more accomplished riders? Does nervousness make you go off course?

My early role models included horsemen who took pride in the quality of their gear, the maintenance of their horses, and their versatility as trainers. They were influenced by California's vaquero traditions of horsemanship.

• Relationships. Do you get into fights with your parents, spouse, or trainer? Do you often find yourself engaged in feuds, or carrying grudges? Does your concern over meeting other people's needs keep you from concentrating on your horse and your rides?

• Self-talk and self-image. Do you beat yourself up for mistakes instead of learning from them and moving on? Is your mind occupied by negative thoughts, such as "I'll never get it right!" or "my horse is just so stupid!"? Does it bother you to ride in front of other people because you're sure they'll criticize or laugh at you?

Every time you answered "yes" to one of those questions, you identified something that interferes with your ability to focus in competition. When you find a way to overcome these kinds of liabilities—for instance, by getting help from a pro trainer or a sports psychologist—you give yourself a significant competitive edge over those who don't.

Becoming a Trainer

Key to success: You have to want it more than anything else in the world.

To succeed at horse training as a career, you need more than a love for horses and the desire to be paid for riding them all day. You have to put your career ahead of everything else, and at times it'll be hard to do. This is a business where "making it" isn't easy.

As a young trainer trying to get established, you'll have next to no personal life. Training horses is a 24-hour, 8-days-a-week job in which you have total responsibility for other people's horses.

You'll miss a lot of holidays, birthdays, and graduations. If you do decide to have a family, your choice of career will be very hard on those loved ones at times. You'll probably come to a better understanding of why some trainers' family relationships don't survive the demands of the career.

But if being a trainer is what you want more than anything else in the world, I'd be the last person to throw cold water on your dream. Training horses can be a rewarding way to make a living if you go about it right.

The right way is the hard way. Do whatever you have to do to get as much hands-on horse experience as possible, as early in life as you can. (If you want to be a show horse trainer, for example, it'll be a definite advantage for you to have shown extensively as a youth or non-pro.)

Then go put your time in as an apprentice to a trainer who's already established a solid career in the performance area that interests you. Don't expect to learn all there is to learn in a few weeks or months. In my program, I want apprentices who'll commit to working for me for four or five years, because that's how long it takes me to train

When I was growing up in the West Coast horse scene of the 1950s and 1960s, horse training was more of a lifestyle than a profession. That's changed. In fact, the degree to which the horse industry has become professionalized, at all levels, is the biggest change to the industry I've seen in my lifetime.

STRAIGHT TRUTH

The horse business is so strong today that anyone who can ride and has half a brain can hang out a shingle, get horses to train, and a group of lesson customers. That person might not make a huge living, but he or she can survive well. It's a tougher deal if you want to get to the top of the hill, because there are a lot of good hands out there today. This is where total focus comes in. It's what separates the consistently winning world-level trainers from the rest of the pack.

them well enough to succeed in their own businesses.

In my opinion, there's just no other way to get the kind of start it takes to succeed in the training business. A college degree is a great thing to have (and you'd be smart to

Earning your spurs, paying your dues, working your way into the outfit—the horse world has many clichés that express a central truth: You can't succeed without earning respect, and to do that, you have to work that much harder than the rest.

get one). Nevertheless, you can't build a career as a professional horse trainer solely by reading books and doing well on tests, any more than you could become a competent surgeon that way.

It's not easy to be a trainer's apprentice, especially when you work for someone who's actually made it to the top tier in any discipline. As a rule, these established trainers are very driven and demanding—I certainly am—and expect that you give them 100-percent-plus.

As an apprentice, you won't get paid to learn; you'll get paid to work. Whatever instruction you receive will be a fringe benefit for performing tasks your boss doesn't have time to do. Based on the inquiries I receive from aspiring trainers, there's considerable misunderstanding about this fact. You'll find the environment to be a lot more like boot camp than day camp, and the glamour to be pretty scarce.

Working for a trainer requires more hard manual labor than most wanna-be apprentices expect. When you're not riding, you'll be on your feet helping with all the work it takes to keep a professional horse operation going. You'll stack hay, clean stalls, fix fences, lug tools, and maybe wash the boss's truck on top of it. You may not get to ride at all until you've proven you can cut it at the other tasks.

You'll need stamina. As a trainer's apprentice, you'll get up early and work until dark, at least six days a week. You'll work outdoors in all kinds of weather. And you won't get rich on the wages. In many cases, you might make more by taking burger orders at McDonald's.

But if you're one of those who can meet the challenge of learning the horse-training profession from the ground up, you'll find life to be a whole lot easier once you do go out on your own. All your years of being a grunt finally will pay off, because you'll start out with a business foundation already in place.

Here's how. You'll have gotten experience in working with all kinds of owners as well as all kinds of horses. You'll be networked in with the other pros your boss respects, and they'll open a lot of doors for you as time goes by.

At some point during your pursuit of a goal, you'll have to make a choice between remaining in your comfort zone, or spurring yourself to go farther than you thought you could. If you win without work, it's not success. It's luck.

You'll have made connections that will get you the better horses, which in turn will help make your name. You'll know something about how to put horse deals together, and have sources of horses to sell.

You'll also have had a taste of the pressures at the top—a big asset if that's where you want to end up in your own training business.

Raising Horses

Key to success: *Your broodmares must be the very best you can buy.*

Today, with the strong prices we're seeing for western performance prospects, more and more people are getting into the breeding aspect of horses. And the biggest hole I see in their programs is their lack of exemplary mare power.

Instead of owning one or two great mares and building a program around them, they'll pour resources into several mares who are average or below what's become the standard for excellence. Either that, or they'll breed mares chosen on the basis of personal attachment rather than top quality.

That's not how you win at this game—especially these days, when it's gotten so much more competitive than it was even five years ago. The business of raising and selling prospects has been revolutionized in ways that have made a foal's dam the deciding factor in salability.

Though the horse industry always has had niches of value and price, there are more "niches within the niches" now than ever before. Yet even in this age of specialization, long-term success comes easiest to those who, like stallion station owner Norm Bryant, become horsemen first, specialists second.

Consider the following points.

• The availability of transported semen has made great sires available to anyone. As a result, it isn't hard for the buyers of prospects to find some who are by top stallions. They sift through them by focusing on the dams.

• Extended pedigrees, performance records, and production histories are increasingly available from association Web-sites and CD-ROMs. This has made buyers much more knowledgeable and, in turn, that much pickier. Technology has given them a way to com-

pare dams on paper or on a computer screen before they ever pick up the phone to call about the offspring you have for sale.

• Horses are increasingly being sought and sold over the Internet, and search capabilities get more sophisticated by the day. The easier it's become for horse buyers to make narrowly specific searches, the more specific they've become with selection criteria.

• The select prospect sales held in conjunction with major events have taken on new importance. Not only have they gotten to be a showcase of outstanding livestock, giving buyers a chance to compare numerous top prospects in the flesh at one time, they've also educated buyers on levels of dams and

how much to pay for their offspring. All other things being equal, buyers know they won't have to pay as much for the prospect whose dam is a granddaughter or great-granddaughter of a well-regarded sire, as they will for the one whose dam was a direct daughter.

Beyond owning outstanding mares, you'll be most successful as a market breeder by breeding to popular, well-promoted stallions—stallions with "brand name" recognition, and whose offspring are eligible for major incentive plans and futurities.

That recognition factor and the value-added programs will cost more in terms of the stud fee you'll pay. However, they'll also make your resulting foals that much more valuable and desirable when they go on the market against other prospects.

If you have to go into a long explanation of who your foal's sire was because most people have never heard of him, you'll automatically reduce the price you can get for that foal. The few hundred dollars you might have saved on a stud fee can cost you a lot more than that at sale time.

Standing a Stallion

Key to success: *You must go the extra mile in every aspect of your operation.*

It's not the mares who decide which stallions they get bred to; it's the people who own the mares. Therefore, without satisfied mare

When breeders fail to make money on the horses they're raising, it's usually because they haven't started with a carefully thought-out plan for providing what the buying public wants. One superior broodmare will yield a greater profit over time than three mediocre ones.

owners in adequate numbers, you won't be in the stallion-service business for long.

When you stand a stallion to the public, it's important to remember that you aren't just selling semen. You're also dealing with people's hopes and egos, and their right to exert choice. To win here, you'll need dedication and plenty of it, because this is an intensely customer-service-oriented endeavor.

Breeding mares is a very monotonous business that ties you down completely. I learned this years ago, working for my father, Don Avila, when he stood the Quarter Horse stallion Docs Dee Bar. That's one reason why stallion stations exist; many stallion owners simply can't make the full-time commit-

ment that breeding season requires.

When you're not checking mares and babies, you'll be collecting stallions, answering the phone, getting semen shipments on their way, or any of a hundred other daily chores. You can't count on getting days off, or even on getting regular sleep, especially if you'll be foaling out mares.

Most people are not prepared for what it costs to promote a stallion. Training bills and entry fees are just the small change that gets you started. If your goal is to make your horse into a household name, you must advertise constantly. A full-page ad once a year in your breed journal won't cut it. You'll need professional-level photos and ad designs, and

I've learned much about horses with heart from my association with Peppy Badger Chex (left) and Lenas Wright On ("Ned," right). Peppy won his second world championship after coming back from a bowed tendon. Ned, who made a 1½ -point error at the start of his NRHA Futurity run, dug in to make up for it and win when I called on him.

you'll need to keep your stallion paid up into major incentives and futurities. I won't pull any punches; this takes a steady source of cash flow.

Running a breeding operation has extremely high requirements for facilities maintenance. You're always going to be fixing or replacing something, and people will notice when you don't keep up.

In most people's minds, a breeding facility needs to have a hospital-like atmosphere, carefully maintained and clean. No one wants to leave his mare at a dirty, broken-down place, but he'll sure tell the rest of the world about it if he finds out that's exactly what you have.

When the horse industry is good, you can make a lot of money by owning and standing a stallion. Notice that I didn't say easy money, because the breeding business is a lot of work.

And, when the horse industry cycles downward, as it does from time to time, breeding is one of the first things to be cut. Keep that in mind when you decide how deeply to invest in the realities of owning and standing a stallion.

tool

MIND PICTURE

Think of your competition skills as links in a chain you'll use for pulling yourself to the top. Then realize that your chain's only as strong as its weakest link.

analysis

Take a Look Inside Yourself

For anyone who wants to reach a goal, self-awareness is an important asset. Use this list of questions to increase yours—you may be surprised at what you'll learn about yourself. Tip: Write your answers down. That'll give you a reference point for developing an improvement plan.

My chosen horse activity is

_____
_____
_____
_____
_____
_____

My long-term goal is to

_____
_____
_____
_____
_____
_____

1. How good at my chosen activity (riding/competing/breeding/training/selling/other) am I now? (Poor, fair, average, above average, great?)

2. How good would I like to be?

3. In the past, why haven't I progressed as I would have liked? (Name all obstacles you can think of.)

4. Am I self-disciplined? (Do I ride regularly? Do I take care of my stock, gear, and facilities the best I can? Do I take advantage of available clinics, lessons, books and videos, seminars?)

5. In the time I devote to my horse activities, do I concentrate on what I'm doing—or do I rush, daydream, or spend a lot of time socializing?

6. Do I take responsibility for my level of achievement—or do I tend to blame others (parents, judges, spouse, trainer, horse) when things go wrong?

7. What skills and resources

If your look at yourself reveals a weakness or a shortcoming, don't waste energy on denials or apologies. Instead, figure that you've just done yourself a favor by pinpointing a problem area, then get to work on fixing it.

must I have to succeed at my horse activity?

8. Which skills and resources am I missing at present?

9. Do I understand and make the effort to keep up with changes in the rules, regulations, and prevailing trends of my chosen activity? If not, what additional measures could I take?

10. In what ways do my emotions hinder me?

11. What do I do best in relation to my horse activity?

12. What do I do the poorest?

13. Do I know how to go about improving my weaknesses? If not, who could help me?

14. Do I deliberately work on improving weak skills—or do I just tend to rehearse what I already do well?

15. How much time per day do I devote to my horse activity now?

16. Is that amount of time adequate? If not, what measures could I take to increase the time I spend?

17. Am I resourceful and persistent about seeking answers to problems—or

do I just ignore them and hope they'll go away?

18. Am I willing to do the extras it takes to be successful? (Budgeting, increasing practice time, consulting pros, attending seminars, culling and upgrading stock, etc.)

19. Have I analyzed the true financial cost of my goal? (Gear and equipment, facilities, lessons and training, advertising, travel, entry fees, etc.)

20. Am I able and willing to budget for that amount, even if it means cutting back in other areas?

With Selective Horse Buying

I'VE LOST track of the number of horses I've purchased over the years, but I haven't lost sight of one fact that was hammered into me long ago by horsemen I respect:

The quality of your horse determines the heights you'll reach. Compromise when you make your purchase, and nine times out of ten, you've just compromised your goal.

As you know if you've ever shopped for a horse, there are many, many variables you have to consider, not the least of which is price. Yet no matter how cheap or expensive a horse might be, I've found that I make my best choices by sticking with one hard-and-fast rule:

If I have to talk myself into liking a horse—if he doesn't make me say, "Wow, I want to own this one!" from the first time I lay eyes on him—I walk away and keep looking.

A huge part of my horse business is based on showing and selling, and I've learned that if a horse doesn't jump up and grab me on first impression, he probably won't do it with judges or buyers, either. This makes the showing or selling task that much harder, and I'd rather not start out with the handicap.

A horse doesn't have to be in tip-top condition for me to buy him, because that's something I can change once I own him. However, a horse does have to be inherently pretty before I'll consider him. If he doesn't have

There's an old saying ...

You win or lose the day you buy your horse.

eye appeal, I'm not interested. When you ride a pretty horse into the show pen before a panel of judges, or lead him out of his stall for a prospective buyer (who's also in judging mode at that moment), you make winning or selling that much easier for yourself.

Beyond that, here's how I'd advise you if you came to me for help in buying western performance type horses for various purposes. I'll aim my advice at the top levels of the marketplace, because that's where standards for quality are established.

Three months after the photo at left was shot, Smart Zanolena won the 1999 GMC Sierra World Championship Snaffle Bit Futurity and a check for $100,000. Even in his everyday tack, he displays that "something extra" I look for in a show or breeding horse.

I own one broodmare without a show record of her own. She produces quality foals, but I don't expect to get as much for them as I do for the foals out of mares who are proven performers. Once her earliest foals prove themselves, her later ones will be worth more.

Broodmares

Buyer's tip: Invest in quality instead of numbers.

Today, quality in a performance broodmare begins with popular, lasting breeding—not just something that's popular today, but that's withstood the changes of style, and the rise and fall of various events' popularity.

The Doc Bar lines are a good example. They've gone from success in halter and western pleasure to winning at cutting, reining, working cow horse, roping, barrel racing, and just about any other performance event you can name. There's a reason why the Doc Bars are still in demand, even though Doc Bar himself has been gone for many years.

But don't just go out and buy mares that have a certain name on their papers. Just because a mare has Doc Bar or any other famous stallion on the far right side of her registration certificate doesn't necessarily mean she'll be a good broodmare. The rest of her pedigree could consist of horses nobody's ever heard of or cares about, or who have done nothing else their entire lives except stand out in the pasture.

When you buy a mare without contemporary market credentials, no matter how cheaply you can pick her up, you automatically reduce both the market for her foals and the price you can get for them. Results from any auction of performance-bred horses will prove this to be true.

It's different if you're looking at a mare who's by, say, Smart Little Lena, who was sired by Doc O'Lena, who was by Doc Bar. In this case, having Doc Bar on the mare's papers is significant, because both Smart Little Lena and Doc O'Lena are proven sires and household names within the performance-horse industry. When someone comes along to look at that mare's offspring, a printout of her sire-line accomplishments will be impressive.

The bottom side of a broodmare's pedigree is every bit as important as the top side. The better her credentials there, the more interested buyers will be in her babies. Was the mare's dam by a proven, well-known stallion? Did the mare's dam ever win anything? Has she produced winners of anything? These are questions that today's buyers of performance prospects have learned to ask, which means you need to be asking them too.

The next aspect of quality in a broodmare is determined by her own show and/or production record. Look for a mare who either won a lot in her own career, or who's produced at least one winner. If you can't get that, look for a full sister of a mare who's won or produced something. It's not just the claim to fame you're after, but evidence of tested and proven performance genetics.

I can't put enough stress on how impor-

At its upper level, the market for broodmares is escalating in value and demand. A quality broodmare such as the one being handled here by Carmen Bryant is seldom offered for sale. When a quality broodmare does become available, she doesn't last long on the market.

STRAIGHT TRUTH

It's been said that great men have great mothers. I think the same can be said of great horses.

tant this factor will be to your breeding program. Anymore, the first question buyers ask when they call about a performance prospect is, "What's the mother done?" If you have to make excuses for her lack of record, chances are good that the buyer will move on to the next prospect on his list. That's really likely if you've priced your mare's offspring the same as ones out of mares with records.

Where do I look for broodmares? Everywhere. I don't necessarily go to farms that are known for great broodmares, because owners who have great broodmares know what they've got and don't sell them. (The exception might be the very old mare whose future producing years are numbered, or in the case of personal crisis, like a death or divorce.)

Because my customers and I breed horses with the intention of producing show horses, I look for retiring show mares, with the hope that they can become great broodmares. I know I'll be gambling on what they'll produce, but I work to reduce my gamble by insisting on certain criteria.

Besides a solid show record, I want a broodmare prospect to have had longevity in the show pen, without a history of complicated soundness problems. I want her to have been

a good young performer, too, because that increases the odds that she won't be one of those mares who produce late bloomers.

I want the mare to have the same pedigree qualities I outlined above—good on both sides—and then I check to see if she has any brothers or sisters who have performed, and if her dam has produced anything noteworthy except this one mare. Some families are more consistent than others in producing performers, and I want as much proof of that as I can get in a broodmare prospect. I won't take a chance on a mare who's basically a freak of nature.

If you're shopping for a broodmare on a limited budget, you can buy an old mare with a production record cheaper than you can a young mare with a show record. I'd definitely buy the old mare instead of a young one with neither kind of record, because her foals will be easier to market.

You do have to keep in mind that you're gambling with fertility, resale value, and longevity. An old mare can be difficult to settle and keep in foal; decline in fertility is one reason why good older mares come up for sale in the first place.

Also, if an old mare fails to settle once you own her, her resale value will be low. If you keep her, the day will come when she has to be put down, and you'll need to be prepared to face that.

SUCCESS LESSON

When you're shopping for horses, it always pays to be patient. I can think of one buying trip when I'd gone from farm to farm without seeing a single yearling that rang my bell. Just when I was about to write the trip off as a complete disappointment, I made one last stop and watched a group of eight or nine stud colts out in a breeder's field. Two of the colts popped right out by the way my eye kept going back to them. Besides having the look and kind of breeding I like, they also loped better than the other colts in the field and had the mellowest attitudes. I ended up buying both.

Stallion Prospects

Buyer's tip: *When you're shopping for a stallion prospect, be aware that the trend in western performance horses is toward level-neck conformation, no matter what the event. I avoid a horse with a naturally upright neck and high head carriage.*

If you think you want to own a stallion, you have to sit down and decide first if you're looking for a breeding stallion, or for the thrill of having a show horse who might make a breeding stallion later on. If you're actually looking for a stallion to stand, you can buy a mature stallion who's achieved an attractive record—a "pre-made" breeding prospect—for much less money than what it actually costs

to buy a top-ticket yearling or 2-year-old and get him to that point.

When I quiz people about their stallion-buying intentions, I find that most are looking for the thrill. They love the idea of having their colt be the next big futurity champion, and of being able to follow and root for him all the way. The idea of buying an older stallion doesn't turn them on—which is fine.

But when you decide to take the thrill-seeker route, you need to know that this is the riskiest and most expensive way to get yourself a prospective breeding stallion. Some colts work and some don't. Some go lame, some get sick, and some just flat don't pan out.

When I'm in the market for a long year-ling or 2-year-old colt to train and campaign for a customer who's hoping to end up with a breeding stallion, paper catches my eye first. If I like the way a colt is bred, I'll go look at him in person. If the horse strikes me as something special when I first see him, I'll continue to be interested.

Maybe he moves in a way that makes me really want to watch him, or is exceptionally pretty. There'll be something about him that says, "I'm a little different from all the rest." That quality, whatever it is, will help him stand out when he starts competing, first for prize money or points, and later for mares.

Double Decked Chex, by Peppy Badger Chex and out of a Smart Little Lena daughter, exemplifies the "pretty" factor that's become a standard in the performance horse world. Double Decked Chex has eye appeal from any angle, posing or in action.

STRAIGHT TRUTH

Prospect shoppers compare what's available, and it's not their problem when your performance prospect's dam doesn't compare well. It's your problem, and you created it the day you bought or bred the mare.

I'll pass on the colt who's nasty or evil-tempered. If I'm going to have a stallion, I want a good-natured one—a horse anyone can handle. When you stand a stallion, a good-natured one sells himself. If he passes that temperament on, people can get something done with his offspring, and that will help him build his sire record that much faster.

When I'm shopping for a mature stallion, one of the biggest things I look for is one who had raw athletic talent when he was started. To find that out, I make a point of tracking down the people who were around the horse early in his training and asking if he showed early talent or not. In my experience, these are the stallions who reproduce athletic talent, which is a heritable trait.

Some stallions who have managed to earn a performance record are little more than the product of a trainer's skill and a customer's willingness to keep spending money. They were able to tolerate being trained and hauled from event to event until they finally became show horses. These individuals seldom make outstanding sires.

People sometimes ask if I'd buy the unshown mature full brother of an established stallion as a prospective breeding horse. I wouldn't, because I think this kind of horse is almost impossible to market well to the public. That's just my opinion, but it's something I feel very strongly about.

You'll hear people justify the purchase of such a horse by saying, "He could have won as much as his brother, but he got injured during training," or "He was just as good as So-and-So, but didn't have the money behind him to prove it."

When you get right down to it, who really cares? The justifications won't make his foals sell better. You can whip the sad story out on everybody in the world, and maybe there are a few people who'll buy into it. But you'll have a hard time establishing a profitable breeding business around a stallion who has to be marketed on the basis of "what could've been" as opposed to "here's what he did."

This yearling filly being longed by assistant Travis Wigen is an excellent example of a naturally flat-necked horse, desirable in nearly all aspects of the current western show-horse market. I look for this type of profile when I'm traveling the country to look for prospects.

Smart Sliden Lena, full brother of
NRHA Futurity champion Lenas
Wright On, has a promotable record
of his own.

insight

MIND PICTURE

You wouldn't expect to dig up a diamond in a sandbox in your back yard— you'd go to a diamond dealer. Think the same way when you're searching for a trained show horse.

Yearling Prospects

Buyer's tip: *You can do a lot to educate your eye for yearlings by going to one of the major breeding farms or a select yearling sale— not with intent to buy, but to compare lots of horses in one place. Pay attention to what grabs you and what doesn't. Then carry those mental pictures with you when you finally do shop to buy.*

You take a bigger gamble with a yearling as a performance prospect than you do with a started 2-year-old, because you really can't tell how a horse will ride until he's actually being ridden. Sometimes you'll pay less money for a yearling than a started 2-year-old, and you just have to weigh that against your risk.

When I do shop the yearling crop, I'm still hunting for the horse with that "something special" to go along with good breeding on both sides. I find it in maybe one out of twenty yearlings I see, so I know that most of my trips to look at specific horses are going to end up as dry runs. I don't let that keep me from continuing to look, though, because you never know when you'll walk out to someone's yearling pasture and hit the jackpot.

The more pedigree-and-records homework you do on a yearling before you make an appointment to see him, the better idea you'll have on whether he's priced fairly for what he is. Breeders whose yearlings are "good on both sides" want good money for them, which is deserved.

But you'll also find yearlings for sale who are by top stallions and out of mares who are only so-so. If they're priced the same as the yearlings with two good sides on their pedigrees, you're not getting a good buy.

Is it a good buy if the price is reduced? Maybe, maybe not. You have to remember that it'll cost just as much in money and time to train the cheaper prospect as it will the more expensive one. And when all is said and done, the less-well-bred prospect won't bring as much at resale time as the better-bred one.

When it comes to buying performance prospects, I don't have a preference between colts and fillies. Outstanding is outstanding, regardless of gender. When I find a prospect who interests me, I develop a program for the individual, and go from there.

One of the biggest "buyer beware" circumstances in the horse industry occurs when you're shopping for a trained show horse. I won't buy one without having seen him be shown, because I want to be sure he doesn't cheat the rider in the show ring.

Trained Show Horses

Buyer's tip: *Don't buy any candidate until you've actually seen him shown.*

That's the most important advice I can give to anyone who's shopping for a trained show horse. The only way you'll know how honest a horse is in the show pen is to observe him in that setting. Don't take the seller's word on the subject. See for yourself if the horse is pleasant in the arena and does what the rider asks without cheating or getting mad.

That's a big part of having a showable show horse, right there. Some show horses are for sale because they're not showable any more. They're ring-sour, ring-smart, ring-cheaters, or whatever else you care to call them. You want those to stay someone else's problem.

You can be seriously misled watching a horse being ridden at his regular home, and people are misled by this all the time. Not realizing that horses eventually figure out

when they're in the show arena and when they're not, buyers will hear about an out-of-state horse who's earned a lot of show points and take an exciting trip to try him out at the owner's or trainer's place. After the horse performs beautifully in his home environment, the buyers will happily fork over the purchase price and not know that their new horse cheats in the show pen until they find out the hard way.

I'm actually wary of the for-sale show horse who's accumulated a pile of points, because to me, it's a red flag that he may be used up. The exceptions—the true-blue show horses who will just keep going and going for years without getting sour—seldom come up for sale unless the owner's going to college or making some other big life change. You can't find one of those deals every day.

Instead, I look for horses who, for one reason or another, haven't been shown more than a few times. Maybe the owner didn't

have the time or money to show him a lot, or took time off to start a family. Maybe he saved him to show a couple of times a year at special events. Whatever the reason, that "low mileage" is something I'm after. The fewer times a horse has been in the show pen, the fewer chances he's had to learn how to cheat.

Unless you're a professional horseperson with a well-honed eye and list of trusted contacts, don't try to buy a trained show horse on your own. It's a very good way to get burned. Enlist a pro to help you. You might pay a little more, but you'll also reduce your risk.

Resale Prospects

Buyer's tip: A pretty horse helps resell himself. Don't settle for less when you buy.

A good-sized segment of the horse industry is made up of people, including myself, who buy horses with the intent of reselling them at a higher price after adding more training or condition. Since there's no shortage of horses available for sale, for any purpose and in every price range, how does a sharp resale buyer sort through them?

Here's one of those learned-the-hard-way lessons:

You should never buy anything for resale that you're not willing to live with for the rest of your life.

I know how tempting it can be to buy a horse on the basis of a cheap price. In the past I've gone ahead and talked myself into buying certain horses just because I thought I could make a buck on them.

That method of choosing resale prospects has almost always ended up biting me in the butt. When a horse's best feature is that he's cheap, low price usually remains his most attractive feature. That doesn't bode well for you in the profit-making department.

I've been a lot more successful with my resale projects ever since learning to ask the "could I see myself keeping him forever?" question. It's been my experience that when you can say yes—truthfully, without apologies or justifications—you've found a resale prospect with inherent value to a buyer. Chances are you won't be the last buyer who'll recognize that value and be willing to pay for it.

Because horses' bodies change so much between birth and rideable age, foals and weanlings are among the riskiest of performance-prospect purchases. I'd rather pay more for an individual as a long yearling than buy him earlier for less, since I'll get a closer idea of what I'll end up with.

advice

Beware of a Bad-Minded Horse

No matter what purpose you have in mind for a horse, I recommend that you turn thumbs down on any purchase prospect who shows himself to be inherently bad-minded. If you already own such a horse, the best thing you can do is get rid of him. You can't change what's inborn, and you can't do anything well without a good-minded horse. The following traits are signs of a bad-minded horse. Watch out for them.

1. The horse communicates with threatening body language that says he'd rather be left alone than be handled. He pushes against you, lays his ears back, swings his rear end toward you, or offers to kick or bite when you come near him. He's always "growly."

2. He has a bad temper and shows it. When you ask him to do something he doesn't want to do, he either sulls up or blows up instead of complying.

3. He pins his ears constantly.

4. He's persistently switchy with his tail. This often goes along with the pinny-eared trait, and in my experience, you can't train either one out.

5. The horse has frequent "brain short-outs" that cause him to explode for no apparent reason, even on familiar turf. You never feel that you can trust him.

6. He insists on walking all over you, with total disrespect for your attempts to get him out of your space. (Note: A horse with this trait may not be inherently bad-minded. Often, he simply was raised as a spoiled pet who always was allowed to have his own way. Sometimes you can get a horse over this with competent, consistent handling, and sometimes you can't. If he doesn't show improvement within 30 days of your effort, chances are he never will.)

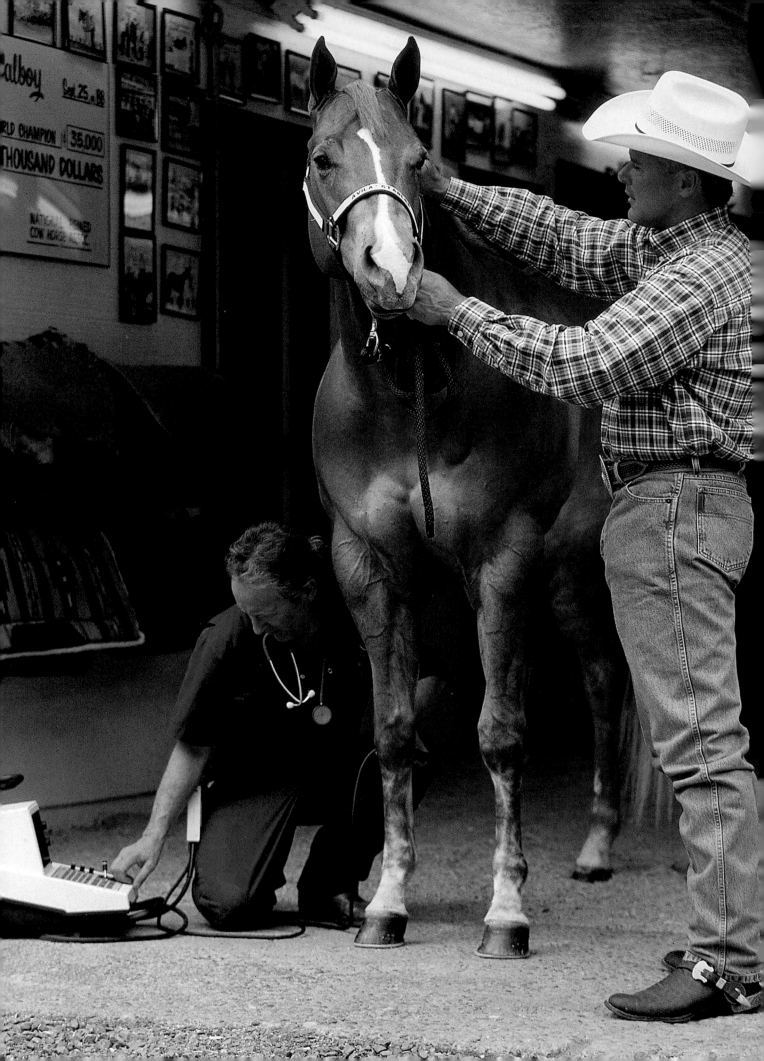

With Your Network of Allies

IN ALL the years I've been involved in the horse business, I've never met anyone who became successful without help from others. Every achiever has a good team behind him, and good teams seldom come together by accident. They're the result of deliberately built relationships. I'm not talking about using people for what you can get, but about investing the effort to develop connections based on mutual respect and trust. Without these, you have no allies, and without allies, you can only go so far.

My point is that since we're all dependent on relationships with other people, we might as well work to make those relationships as good as they can be, after making sure we're partnered up with the right people to start with.

At minimum, your list of allies needs to include a dedicated vet and farrier. In my opinion, most people also will benefit from some sort of relationship with a professional trainer. The list goes on from here, depending on your setup and situation.

For example, unless your horses are boarded, you'll need such allies as feed and bedding suppliers you can count on. You'll need competent barn helpers—if nothing else, a reliable horse-sitter at vacation time. If you're a pro trainer you'll need good working relationships with your customers, as well as with other trainers and your own assistants.

There's an old saying ...
You're only as good as your help.

Your family relationships come into play here, too, and so do your relationships with friends, fellow competitors, and everyone else who might possibly affect your goal.

You'll do yourself a favor by analyzing your key relationships. There's a worksheet at the end of this chapter for that purpose. Meanwhile, here are more of my thoughts on certain kinds of alliances.

"You scratch my back, and I'll scratch yours." Horses benefit from that idea, and so do successful horse people. You can go much farther with the aid of others than you can by yourself. Veterinarian Eric Witherspoon, shown tending to halter gelding Coolest Man Around, is one of my valued allies.

49

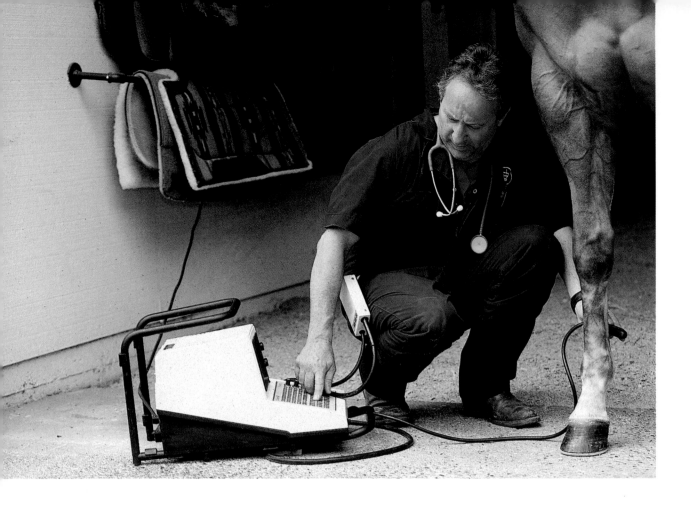

At some point in your pursuit of a goal, its success or failure will rest in the hands of your veterinarian or farrier. (Right, farrier Don Hook scrutinizes his work on one of my horses.) Choose these partners with deliberate care, pay them promptly, and treat them as members of your team.

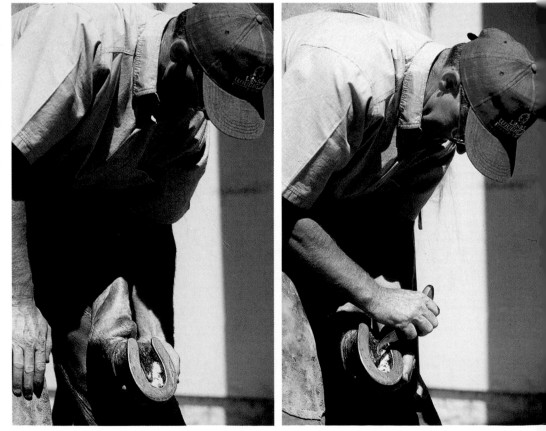

Veterinarian and Farrier

Best advice: *Choose your vet and farrier as carefully as you would your own health-care providers.*

Your choice of veterinarian can be a matter of life and death, literally, and your horses are only as good as their hoof care. This makes your vet and farrier absolutely critical to the success of your horse program. That may seem obvious, but believe me, it's a fact that blows right on by some people. I am constantly amazed by the number of horse owners who shortchange themselves here.

Ask around for recommendations, and if you're not satisfied with the first vet or farrier you try, try someone else. When you do find a vet and farrier you click with, make sure you hold up your end of the relationship with prompt payment and by having your horses ready at appointment time. Schedule enough regular visits with these professionals to make them more than names in your phone book. The

better they get to know you and your horses, the better care you're bound to get.

If you were to ask me what I look for in the vet and farrier who'll get my regular business, my answer would be the same for both.

First, I want someone who cares a lot about what he's doing, and who's not in business just to make a buck. I hate to say this, but as with any profession, the veterinary and horse-shoeing professions do include some individuals whose biggest concerns are their own schedules and bottom lines. You don't have to have done much business with a person before you can spot the difference.

Next, I want my vet or farrier to be someone who's not afraid to say, "I'm in over my head on this one. I need help. Let's call in some reinforcements." I want the person who's open-minded about solving problems, and who doesn't automatically dismiss my ideas just because I didn't go to school in his field. A lot of times, the person who rides and cares for a horse daily knows that horse in a way that the vet or farrier can't.

It's important to me to have motivated problem-solvers on this part of my team. One of the best vets I ever had (until his health forced him to retire) simply would not rest until he'd found the answer to a problem, or at least something new to try. He was aggressive in his pursuit of new information, a trait that all great vets (and farriers) share.

SUCCESS LESSON

When it comes to hiring help, I learned something from a customer over 20 years ago that's been valuable to me ever since. The customer, Ken Austin, owned a large dental-supply company. His office faced the parking lot—kind of a strange spot for the "big gun"—or so I thought until he told me why he'd picked that office. He said that by overlooking the parking lot, he could see the condition of people's cars when they arrived to apply for jobs. He didn't care if the cars were new, but he did care how well they were kept, because it said something about the owners and their self-pride. I think about that story every time someone drives up to my place to apply for work.

Barn Help

Best advice: *This is like hiring anyone else. You need to use your head and not just hire the first person who drops in off the street.*

"Barn help" is a broad category, because every operation differs in what needs to be done. For instance, there's the Mom-and-Pop operation with five or six horses, whose barn-help needs can be met by someone who'll clean stalls for an hour or two a day. Then you have the ranches like mine, where the need for barn help is constant, requiring several full-time employees.

No matter what you need done, I'm sure you want people who are dependable and trustworthy, and who'll take good care of

I would be leery of doing business with anyone who has trouble keeping employees. Pablo Gomez, who heads up my barn-help crew, has been with me for about 15 years. It's hard for me to imagine running my operation without him.

your property. So do I. When I'm deciding on who to hire, I put a lot of faith in first impression. If I'm going to be entrusting my horses and my place to someone, I want that person to display evidence of self-pride. This gives me some indication that the person takes pride in his or her work.

I'm impressed by good personal grooming, clothes that are clean and in good repair, and a clean car or truck. I'm turned off by the opposite. I realize that barn work is dirty by nature, but when a person's dirty and sloppy before he even starts, I see a red flag.

The way to keep good help once you find it is pretty simple. You just need to treat people the same way you'd want to be treated if you were in their position. Just because a person works with a pitchfork doesn't make him a second-class citizen. When you treat someone with disrespect, that's what you get in return, and that person doesn't stick around. In fact, I think you can tell a lot about someone's character and operation (in any business) by how long he or she has been able to keep help.

Professional Trainer

Best advice: *Cultivate some kind of relationship with a professional horseperson you respect.*

I honestly don't believe you can achieve maximum success in the horse game without the aid of a pro. Even if you're talented enough to train your own horse, prepare him, and get him shown well without help, you still need someone on your team who has a professional's perspective. Otherwise, you'll run the risks of missing important new trends, developing bad riding habits, and making the wrong choices when faced with critical decisions.

You don't necessarily have to keep a horse in full-time training in order to build an alliance with a pro. You can do it by taking lessons or by going to seminars or clinics. Some pros will accept your offer of helping them out from time to time, or allow you to bring a horse over and ride with them once in a while.

Another excellent method of getting to know a pro is to volunteer for some kind of association work. You can serve with a pro on a committee, be a pro's ring steward when he judges, or perform some other duty that'll help a door open for you while you're doing something good for the horse industry.

The whole idea is to make a contact, so you'll have someone to call on when you need to. If that person isn't able to help you, he or she may know someone else who can.

When a pro does give you a helping hand, I think it's good etiquette to offer to pay him or her for the time and advice you received. Most of the pros I know are pretty good-hearted and don't always expect to be paid

STRAIGHT TRUTH

The horse industry has a pretty thick line of bull running through it. When a prospective trainer starts telling you about all the great things he's going to do, instead of what he's done, I'd advise you to run the other direction. Some trainers are a lot better at selling themselves to you than they are at producing results for you.

in these situations. But your offer will be appreciated, whether the pro takes you up on it or not, and you'll be respected for having offered the choice.

Suppose you decide you do want full-time training, but aren't sure who to go with. How do you make the right pick?

I think your best first move is to rely on word-of-mouth. You do have to be open-minded enough to consider the source of your information, so you don't get swept up into a case of sour grapes or rosy-eyed hero worship. But if you'll take it upon yourself to ask around, you'll hear much of what you need to know.

For clues on whether you want to do business with an individual, observe him or her (without introducing yourself just yet) at some public function, like a horse show or other event. Pay attention to how the trainer runs things, cares for the horses, conducts himself or herself with customers and officials, and so on. Then ask yourself if you'd feel comfortable about being part of that picture. If not, you need to keep looking.

If you like what you've heard and seen so far, make a point of going to the pro's place before hiring him or her to train your horse. Some trainers have impressive trappings out in public, yet run stables that are unsafe and dirty. Check out the facility, how it's run, the condition of the horses, and how the train-

er's employees conduct themselves.

Unless you feel 100 percent comfortable about where your horse would be and about the level of care he'd receive, you shouldn't become a customer. You'll always be worried about your horse, putting distrust into the relationship to start with.

When your purpose for hiring a trainer includes competition, I feel very strongly that you need to pick someone who's already proven he or she can compete or coach others successfully at the level you have in mind. Don't select a trainer on the basis of who's closest to you, who's cheapest, or who's got the jolliest personality. What you need is experience, at that level.

That advice holds for anyone, but I'd especially like to make the point to parents who engage professional trainers to work with their kids.

Say you have a child whose dream is to go to a state finals, regional championship, youth world show, or other event. This means stepping up, and to do that successfully, you need to engage a professional who has a record of

When you're in the market for someone to train your horse, pay attention to the way the people you're considering use their hands while riding. I look for evidence of light, sensitive feel in those I hire to ride for me, because I want light response in my horses.

taking youngsters to the event your family has in mind. He or she will know what caliber of horse it takes, what kind of tack and clothing are suitable, how to cope with ground and arena conditions, and all the other nuances of competing there.

You'll hear parents justify their choice of a less-experienced trainer as their upper-level guide by saying, "I don't care if my child wins, I just want her to have fun." I'm not intending to put the less-experienced trainers down in any way, but to help parents make decisions after knowing the full perspective. I've seen so many kids leaving their "big show" feeling completely embarrassed and humiliated by what they didn't know before they got there. How can that be considered fun? To me, it's borderline cruel.

I think the biggest thing to remember when hiring a trainer is that you're buying much more than his or her ability to train horses. You're purchasing (or should be purchasing) a total program that includes the trainer's level of experience, caliber of assistants, manner of treating people and behaving in public, ability to care well for your horse and get bills paid on time, professional network, and good reputation. Your choice of trainer will reflect on you and affect your life in more ways than one.

I'm going to assume for a moment that you've found your ideal trainer, someone who treats you and your horse the way you want, and who's capable of producing the results you seek. Here's what you should expect to contribute in order to make this relationship function well as a two-way street.

Remember that your trainer (or your teacher, riding coach, 4-H club leader, or whoever else is helping you) has a personal life just like you do. A trainer will appreciate you for treating that part of his life with respect—for calling at reasonable hours, for granting privacy at holiday time, for not dropping by unannounced on Sunday mornings, and so forth.

Professionals also have feelings, so if a problem or misunderstanding arises between you and your trainer, talk to him about it directly, before grousing to all your friends. When it comes to gossip, the horse world's very small, and what you've said may come back to haunt you with embellishments you didn't expect.

You'll do your horse goal a lot of good by cultivating some kind of relationship with a pro. If you can't afford to keep your horse in full-time training, take lessons. If that's not possible, look for other ways to get a relationship going, so you have someone to call on when you need help.

STRAIGHT TRUTH

When I hire my apprentices, talent isn't my first priority. The desire to excel comes first. Next, I look for politeness and neatness. Talent comes after that.

To me, it's just common interpersonal courtesy to speak directly to the person with whom you're having the problem. No one likes to get the first inklings about a problem via the grapevine, which these days includes the Internet.

Any businessperson on your list of allies deserves to have his bill paid in a timely fashion. In your trainer's case, he's already put out the money for the feed your horse eats and the care he receives, and relies on steady cash flow to cover operating costs. While I think the majority of people who put horses in training are great about paying their trainers on time and therefore don't even need the subject brought up, I've also had to make enough calls on late payments to know that everyone's not like this.

There's at least one more aspect to maintaining a good relationship with your trainer, and it happens to be one I feel very strongly about: When your hired professional gives you his or her advice or opinion on something, even if it's something you didn't want to hear, you should listen.

If you don't have enough trust in your trainer to do that, I think you need to get a different trainer. This relationship *must* be based on trust in order to work. Great achievers let their advisers advise them, in the horse industry as well as any other.

Assistant Trainers

Best advice: *Hire people who'll represent you and your training business well.*

I've been fortunate over the years to have had good people work for me who've gone on to become outstanding professionals in their own right. They've helped me to become known as someone who can train trainers as well as horses, and that's put me in a position of being able to pick and choose among young hands when I have an opening to fill. But I've also hired some training assistants who didn't last long, and that's taught me to listen to my gut and not overlook something about a person just because I need another hand right away.

In a lot of ways I'd compare my approach to finding an assistant trainer to my search for a show prospect. First impression counts for a lot. If someone rubs me the wrong way right off the bat, I won't even think about hiring that person. It's just like with horses—if something bothers me about an individual, I don't waste time even trying to figure out what it is. I just move on to the next prospect.

My assistants represent my business, so I need employees who are polite, have good manners, and are respectful toward others. Just like anyone else, I'd rather spend my day working with people who have pleasant personalities than with those who are sullen or moody. Most of my customers view their

First impression counts for a lot with me, whether I'm hiring an assistant trainer or deciding which show prospects to put my time into. A person who's polite, clean-cut, and well-groomed gets my attention in a positive way.

time at my barn as recreation time, and it's no fun for them to come out and work with their horses when they have to deal with a disagreeable assistant.

Like with a horse, I also want decent pedigree. For my area of specialty in the horse business, that means someone with a strong hands-on background in handling show horses. A trainer who has enough business to require an assistant usually doesn't have time to teach someone the basics of his specialty. He needs someone who can go right to work with a minimum of supervision.

Because I'm in the show-horse field, I want assistants who have eye appeal. That means someone who's clean-cut and looks good on a horse. This pleasant picture is a show-ring advantage, and since my assistants will eventually show some of my customers' horses, I want that advantage in place from the start.

MIND PICTURE

Think of your network of allies as a web, with you and your horse goal at its center. The more strands you can add to this web with your own contribution to relationships, the bigger the web will be, and the more opportunities you'll catch.

"The look" isn't something I can define. I think you just know it when you see it.

When I watch a person ride, I look for natural ability, which usually reveals itself in how the hands are used. I want someone with a good sense of feel, and whose hands are light because he or she knows how to ride effectively with the rest of the body. This isn't hard to spot when you see it, either.

There's just as much to being a good boss as there is to being a good assistant. For one thing, it's the boss's job to earn the employees' respect by giving clear direction and feedback. I think it's great to be their friend, but a good boss also leaves no doubt who's in charge. I think a good boss considers the assistants' dignity. When I have to set an assistant straight on something, I do it privately 99 times out of a hundred.

In my opinion, the trainer who's a good boss also works to make assistants feel important and like they're an important part of the business. I make it a point to include my assistants when I'm working with customers, other trainers, magazine writers and photographers, industry leaders, or anyone else who's part of my professional world.

I ask for their opinions on things constantly, and not just so they'll learn to think analytically. I also want them to feel included for their input. When I think they're ready, I give them their chance to show the best of my barn's horses.

That might not be the deal that assistant trainers get at every operation, but it's what's always worked best for me. In any relationship, you get back what you give.

As you're building your team of allies, focus on finding people who are positive thinkers and who truly love what they do with horses. Negativity is infectious and can drag both you and your goal down if you aren't careful about avoiding those who are already afflicted with it.

clarify

Create Your List of Allies

Use these 15 self-analysis questions to increase your awareness of key relationships and how you can build or enhance them. If you need to make changes, don't procrastinate.

1. Who's on your team of allies now? (List everyone from helpful friends and family members to paid and unpaid professionals.)

2. What contributions do they make toward your goal?

3. Are those contributions adequate in your eyes?

4. What, if anything, would you like each ally to do better or differently for you?

5. What actions have you taken to communicate this desire?

6. What other actions, if any, could you take to communicate better?

7. In your relationship with each ally, what do you provide in return?

8. Do you believe your contributions to be adequate? Why or why not?

9. What action could you take to make each relationship even better?

10. Which (if any) members of your present team have you considered replacing?

11. What allies do you need that you don't have now?

12. What action could you take to find them?

13. What will you do to get the new relationships off on the right foot?

14. What have you learned from past key relationships, good or bad, that you can apply to your future ones?

15. By doing so, what will be the benefits toward attainment of your goal?

With Excellence in Presentation

WOULDN'T IT be great if you could get your hands on a magical substance that would add at least 10 percent more value to everything you own, including your horses, and that would allow you to get that much more competitive edge from all your horse endeavors? That substance does exist, and you can start to use it today without necessarily spending a dime.

The formula goes by many names, including elbow grease. I think of it as the extra trouble that goes into making any picture or presentation as good as it possibly can be, so it'll stand out in a crowd.

To me, it doesn't matter if the focus is on upkeep of your facilities, gear, and vehicles; the condition of your stock; the image you create in promotional materials; or the way you appear and behave in public. We live in a visual world, where a viewer's immediate impression carries clout.

Whether it's good clout or bad is up to you, based on the effort you do or don't put in. Let's face it, even though nothing exists that can't be enhanced, no one's going to force you to go that extra mile. The majority of people don't do all the extras—but that in itself provides opportunity for anyone who will.

Just about everyone in today's society is feeling pinched for time. Still, whenever I hear someone say, "Hey, I just don't have time to be messing with all the little stuff," I have

There's an old saying ...
The shiniest apple sells first.

to wonder just how badly he or she wants to be a winner. To me, a person either has a reason for managing time and effort effectively, or a million excuses for not doing so. Excuses are easier to create than results, but what do excuses get you besides more lack of results and the unpleasant urge to apologize for them?

In this chapter, I'll reveal more about my approach to the power of presentation. Dig in and help yourself to an edge that will take you out ahead of the pack.

To win with excellence in presentation, you don't need the newest or fanciest things. You just need to put thought and effort into taking good care of what you do have. Remember that you don't get a second chance to leave a positive first impression.

Your Horse Property

In a nutshell: *Keep the place tidy and keep up with the maintenance.*

If you're going to let other horse people onto your property for business purposes, whether it's to buy or board horses, put them in training, breed to your stallion, or take lessons, you'll help yourself by learning to look at your place through strangers' eyes, and by correcting anything that leaves a negative impression.

Otherwise, it's all too easy to get used to living with what others see as eyesores and pains in the you-know-where. If you don't think you can be objective about what others see, ask a friend to help you. You'll usually get an opinion!

I compare any business-conducting horse property to a restaurant, department store, boutique, auto dealership, or any other retail establishment that does face-to-face business with customers. Nobody likes to give his trade to an operation that's hard to find,

dirty, rundown, littered and cluttered, disorganized, filled with grimy inventory, or overrun by obnoxious pets. When a customer does walk into a place like this, he automatically expects to pay a lower price for whatever is for sale.

These reactions are part of basic human nature and easy to understand. Yet I'm always amazed by the number of horse-property owners who don't take full advantage of this knowledge by making their place of business as appealing as it can be. They're only hurting themselves and opening doors for their competition.

You don't need a fancy place in order to impress customers, make them feel comfortable, and spark their urge to come back. No matter how small and modest your horse operation, you'll set it apart from many others just by keeping it clean and in good repair. You'll set it apart even farther if you can manage to store your "someday" projects and materials—those piles of important stuff that others might view as junk—somewhere out of immediate sight.

If your resources allow you to frost the cake with some degree of landscaping and attractive signage, you'll really be far out ahead of the pack, because you'll have created the curbside appeal that so many other horse properties lack. That's important, because a cus-

success

tomer begins to form an impression about what you have to sell long before he walks into your barn or pasture.

Like your place overall, your barn needn't be fancy as long as it's tidy and clean. When a customer sees your halters and blankets hung neatly, your aisleway uncluttered, your tack room organized, and so forth, he can't help but feel that much more comfortable about the integrity of the rest of your program.

I think customers (not to mention workers and horses) also appreciate a barn that's well-lit. I know I'd rather not spend 10 minutes in a dark barn, let alone an entire day. You don't necessarily have to spend a fortune to brighten up your barn. I've been able to brighten mine significantly just by painting the ceiling and stall fronts white and by covering the dirt aisleway with light-colored shavings that reflect light from overhead.

My whole point is that the more pleasant you make your environment, the more pleasant you make your customers' cnvironment while they're doing business with you, and the more likely they'll be to stick around long enough for you to sell them something.

I'm sure we all could tell stories about going to horse places that were not pleasant environments in which to do business, and that left us wanting to get in our trucks and drive off as fast as possible. "Turnoff" horse properties exist at every economic level, bottom

SUCCESS LESSON

Tony Amaral, the trainer I worked for while in my teens and 20s, was someone who really understood how neatness and cleanliness command respect. Tony never drove a dirty truck, and always wore his best hat and a clean shirt to town even if it was just to get gas. At shows, he kept his boots polished and his barn aisle swept, and his sale horses were presented just as immaculately to buyers as his show horses were to judges. There've probably never been as many good cowboy hats in one place as there were at Tony's funeral, and he'd have appreciated that. He was a person who always put his best foot forward in public.

to top, and make you wonder if the people who live there are blindfolded.

I've gone on buying trips, for instance, and had high-dollar horses shown to me off properties where I wouldn't leave a dead dog. I've been sent videos of expensively priced performance prospects shown standing in swampy pens bordered by junked cars and rusted-out horse trailers. I've even looked at yearlings stabled in garages, stuck between the kids' bikes and the parents' cars. Those kinds of jarring first impressions are just about impossible for customers to overcome.

I'll be the first person to admit that it's no

easy task to keep up with the maintenance on a horse property. Horses are hard on things, and it seems like you're always fixing or replacing something. That's why I believe it's really important to the success of your horse enterprise to fix things as they need to be fixed, and to replace them as they need replacing. The longer you put these jobs off, even if there are more fun things to do in your spare time, the faster your place will deteriorate, and the harder and more costly it'll be to get caught back up.

Besides keeping up with repairs, I've made it a rule to budget for some kind of property upgrade project every year. Property improvements are like savings accounts; they can't grow if you don't start them and then feed them on a regular basis. Even if the project's a small one, it helps improve the total picture as long as it's part of a long-term plan and not tossed up haphazardly. One year, for instance, you might install a ranch sign at the end of your drive, then add trees, shrubs, or flowers to the site the following year.

You can take an incremental approach to the improvement of just about anything and come out ahead over time, compared to the person who waits for the perfect opportunity to do everything at once.

Your Sale Horses

In a nutshell: Any sale day is a show day.

As a seller, whether by auction or private treaty, you have greater control over the price your horse brings than you might think. The more you can make him gleam like a polished diamond before a buyer ever lays eyes on him, the more you can get for him. It all goes back to presentation and the value of first impression. Shine sells.

This seems like a no-brainer, right? Yet think back on all the times you've looked at horses for sale, and ask yourself how many of those horses were presented to you with less than perfect grooming and in their everyday tack. If your experience as a buyer has been anything like mine, the unpolished diamonds

Here's a great visual lesson in the power of presentation. These photos, all of the stallion Shining Shoes, depict him fresh from a night in his stall; in his everyday working tack; and turned out as he would be for a competition or initial-look viewing by a prospective buyer. In the first two shots, he's just another nice horse. In the third shot, he has "wow" factor.

have been the norm. The exceptions have stood out and made you appreciate them.

I flip this experience around when I'm on the selling side. From having been a buyer myself, I know that horse shoppers are in a critical, judging mode from the moment they turn into a seller's drive, arrive at an auction, or see the first frame of a sales video. They're just like show judges, except that buyers award you money instead of a blue ribbon for having the first-place horse.

I also know that buyers want to buy something. Every time they actually take the trouble to go look at a horse for sale,

they're hopeful that this trip will end the search. Plus, I'm aware that when they come to look at my horse, they're carrying the mental pictures of every other sale horse they've seen.

To capitalize on this buyer-mode experience, I make sure that a customer's first look at a sale horse takes place when the animal is at his absolute best. No matter what his job is, the horse will walk out of his stall

enhance

MIND PICTURE

Any picture you present is like a hot-air balloon. The more details you leave undone, the more holes get punched in the balloon, and the less likely it is to fly as far as you'd like it to go.

groomed and tacked up to look like the reigning world champion at that job. This makes it easier for the customer to imagine himself as the next proud possessor.

I put every sale horse through the full show-grooming routine. The horse will have been bathed and clipped, his feet will be polished and freshly trimmed or shod, his mane and tail will be combed out and glossed, and he'll be wearing the best of my show gear. Even an old broodmare will get a silver halter to go along with the grooming.

I have a reason for doing this beyond the obvious positive first impression. I want my customers to know that I respect their eye and their time enough to have gone to the trouble of showing them the best picture possible. Even if my horse doesn't suit them and they leave without buying, they'll still have been acknowledged as discriminating horsepeople. From experience that goes back to my childhood, I know that this impression sets well with customers and encourages them to come back.

I also pay close attention to the presentation of stallions I'm associated with. To me, just because your stallion isn't shown any more doesn't mean he no longer needs to be kept up like a show horse. For the mare owners who come to see him, he continues to be a type of show horse every day of his life. He should be the most well-cared-for and proudly displayed animal on the ranch, though this isn't always what you see.

I've heard people say, "It isn't what my stud looks like that's important, it's the number of mares he gets in foal." I disagree with that completely.

Put yourself in the mare owner's place. If you aren't impressed by the stallion you're considering for your mare, you're not even going to give him the chance to get her in foal. Plus, you're probably going to pass on some negative word of mouth after seeing just how bad Joe Blow's stallion looked when you saw him in person.

Photography and Videos

In a nutshell: *It pays to go with the pros.*

You may have heard it said that a photograph is a moment in time. The same could be said of any video going to a prospective buyer. Depending on the care you take in producing these items, they can be either good moments in time or bad ones. The latter will do your program as much harm as good

I learned much about excellence in presentation from watching Don Dodge, one of my childhood idols. He was known as Mr. Class, because everything he did was always first class, plus, plus, plus, with no detail too small for his attention.

STRAIGHT TRUTH

You hear people say, "Pretty is as pretty does," and I am absolutely, 100-percent against that notion. Pretty is pretty, period, and we live in a world where prettiness gives an edge to anything. If that weren't true, there'd be no landscaping at Disneyland.

ones will help it, making this a poor place to cut corners.

I've always found professionally shot photographs to be well worth what they cost to obtain. Not only will a professional equine photographer have the specialized skills, knowledge, and equipment necessary to make your horses look as good as possible, he or she also will know how to produce prints or slides that reproduce well in ads. You can't get either result with photo equipment, digital or not, designed primarily for taking personal snapshots.

If a show photographer gets good shots of your horse during competition, don't pass up the chance to purchase prints. If you need

photos done of your horses at home, consider setting up a "shoot day" and paying a day fee for an equine photographer to come in and photograph several horses in the same session. The money you'll invest in this will repay itself many times over. You

may be able to split the day-fee expense with a neighboring horse owner who needs photos taken, too.

Since most videos are meant for single viewings by prospective horse buyers and aren't reproduced for mass consumption in the way ads and brochure photos are, I don't think having a professional behind the camera is as critical for videos as it is for photographs. The exception might be a promotional video for a ranch or breeding stallion.

However, I think it is important to do professional-level preparation of your horses, having them groomed and tacked up in their "go to town" best before a camera gets near them. Why make the viewer work hard to like your horse? The photos and videos you send out will take the place of a physical first impression, so it's to your benefit to have your horses looking as good as they can.

The same goes for the turnout of anyone who'll appear in the final images with the horses. A handler dressed in pressed jeans and shirt and clean boots leaves a more positive impression, and complements a well-prepped horse better, than someone who's in everyday barn clothes, sneakers, and a ball cap.

It's also important to have your photos or videos shot against pleasant, undistracting backgrounds (no junk piles, no broken-down fences, no manure heaps, etc.), and to do what you can to keep "negative noise," like that of

When a customer brings friends or family members to my ranch to watch his or her horse perform, I'm aware that some measure of that person's pride and ego are on the line. I try to boost both by showing the horse turned out to look his best.

barking dogs, fighting kids, and crying babies, out of your videos. When a horse shopper scrutinizes the materials you've sent, he'll notice everything in the images, not just the horse itself, and will make assumptions about you, your stock, and your program accordingly. These assumptions may lie below the surface of consciousness, but will affect him nonetheless, and may make the difference between the decision to pursue doing business or not.

If your own property doesn't afford you a pleasant background, think about hauling your horses somewhere else to be photographed or videoed. A fairgrounds, trainer's arena, or friend's place might provide you with a better backdrop for all the other work you'll go through to produce appealing images of your stock.

Your Public Image

In a nutshell: Always put your best foot forward.

As a participating member of any horse community, you're on display any time you're out in public. Even when you're merely buying feed or waiting in line at a show office to pay your bill, your behavior, language, manners, and grooming are noticed and evaluated by others. Every impression builds the image by which you become known throughout that community.

What does this have to do with whether

you'll be able to reach your goals with horses? Plenty, especially if you compete or have some kind of horse business. The image you create of yourself away from the show ring or business, good or bad, goes right back to the show ring or business with you, helping or hurting accordingly.

I'll elaborate. What we call the horse industry is really a people industry that keeps no secrets and runs on earned respect and reputation. You can't be rude, obnoxious, backstabbing, or a slob around fellow horsepeople part of the time, and then expect them to respect you the rest of the time. You can't mouth off to your parents, make scenes in show offices, or be intoxicated in public, and

By paying attention to the impressions you leave, you'll help yourself stand out from the pack in a memorable and positive way.

think that no one will notice or remark on your behavior to others.

Here's why. Sooner or later, you will encounter a fellow horseperson with the power to open a door toward your goal, or close it. It could be a judge, a prospective customer, or the most mean-minded gossip in your equine circle. You're not going to get the nod or even the benefit of the doubt from someone when you've already given him or her cause to lose respect for you. If that loss of respect costs you a customer, a recommendation, or half a point on a run that matters, you've just sacrificed an edge you could have kept.

Some people refer to this as "politics," and

have disdain for it. I regard it as a mere fact of human nature, and acknowledge that it matters.

I'm coming at this subject from the perspective of someone who's spent a lifetime observing the horse industry at work and seeing it evolve. For instance, when I was growing up, horse trainers weren't necessarily known to be role models of decorum. Many of the ones I knew were social mavericks who lived hard and played hard, without much care for what others thought. They took pride in their image of being half-wild. Training horses was regarded more as a lifestyle than a business.

This isn't how it is any more. Our entire culture is now heavily influenced by big business and business practices, and that influence has reached the horse world. Today's training customer expects his trainer to dress like a businessperson, talk like one, and act like one. Today's parents won't put their kids with trainers or coaches who have reputations as hard partiers and substance abusers. Today's judges would rather not reward competitors with questionable reputations.

Moms are right; good manners will help you get ahead in life, and it pays to keep your underwear clean.

improve

10 Free (or Nearly-Free) Ways To Gain a 10-Percent Edge

The following projects don't require extraordinary time and effort, yet will help you benefit from the power of presentation. The little extras do add up.

1. Wash your truck-and-trailer rig and clean the interior before you take it out in public. Even if no one notices your efforts, you'll enjoy the pump-up that comes from driving a clean and well-kept vehicle.

2. Schedule a trip to the local landfill to dispose of the junk you've been meaning to get rid of. This is no one's favorite job, but your horse property will be improved automatically.

3. Take part of a day to clean and reorganize your tack-storage area. Besides making it look better, you'll increase efficiency and be reminded of what items need to be repaired or replaced.

4. Ask a friend for input on how you could improve the first-impression, "drive-up" appearance of your place. Your friend will be flattered that you value his opinion, and you may get tips you wouldn't have thought of on your own.

5. Scout your property to find the best site for taking photos of your horses. Take snapshots and scrutinize the backgrounds. If you can't find one that's open and uncluttered, you'll know you need to find an off-site shooting location.

6. If you have dogs, create a place when they can be penned up when guests and customers visit. Chances are other people won't find your pets as appealing as you do, and loose dogs do nothing to clinch a sale or enhance a presentation.

7. Go through horse magazines with a critical eye, looking for examples of unflattering equine photos. Analyze ways the photos could have been improved—better grooming, nicer tack, less junky backgrounds, etc.—then apply the knowledge to your own photo efforts. Do likewise with videos of horses offered for sale by others.

8. Pressure-wash the interior of your barn periodically. By getting rid of accumulated dust and cobwebs, you'll freshen the place up while improving air quality and cutting down on respiratory ailments.

9. Make it a rule to coil up hoses and stow ranch tools after each use. You'll reduce ugly clutter and help your tools last longer.

10. Make several copies of each sale horse's registration papers, show or production records, win photos, etc., and put each set into a separate hand-out folder that also includes your business card. By presenting a set to each person who comes to see each horse, you'll appear organized and businesslike while increasing your chances of getting referrals.

With Quality Gear and Care

I'D BE willing to bet that you find your-self making assumptions about a person when you first lay eyes on his horses. If they're at the peak of health, well outfitted, and managed with quality care, your estimation of the owner probably goes up.

Most of us have some idea of the effort that goes into good equine management, respecting those horsemen who go to the trouble. The opposite is just as likely when we see horses who are lacking in some area of their care.

This is nothing new. Horsemen have been sizing each other up on this basis since ancient times, not just for snob appeal, but as a gauge of power. If your horses were in substandard gear and in poorer health and condition than those of your rivals, you stood to lose most of the battles you faced.

The only difference between then and now is in the winner's spoils. Today, a compromise in your gear and horse care won't cost you the right to control all of France. But it could mean the difference between first and fifth in the event you've been training toward, or be the deciding factor in whether you're able to keep your prospects and performers sound. Since the results are obvious for all to see, compromised horse care definitely hurts you at sale time. And, it does nothing to elevate you in the eyes of your peers.

That's not to say that you shouldn't be concerned about spending your time and money

There's an old saying ...
Penny wise, pound foolish.

wisely on your gear and horse care, or that you can't enjoy success with your horses if you practice certain economies. But there is such a thing as false economy that'll hurt your chance of reaching goals while harming your horse program overall.

That's what I want to help you avoid with the information in this chapter, because it's where many goal-seekers go wrong.

Quality in bits, strap goods, saddles, and other tack is determined by materials and workmanship, not by glitzy trim and faddish style. I still get daily use from tack I invested in over 20 years ago. Good gear doesn't cost. It pays.

I start every horse I train in a ring snaffle, noseband, and running martingale. I go back to this gear whenever I'm reschooling an older horse with performance problems.

Tack and Equipment

Just remember: *The quality of your tools determines the quality of your work.*

I don't know anyone who doesn't enjoy getting a good buy on tack and equipment. There's a big difference, however, between quality gear offered on sale, and gear that's sold cheaply because it's cheaply made. There's also a big difference in the results you can expect to get while riding and training. For my money, I'd rather pay more to get more, because quality gear that lasts and lets a horse work in comfort is always the better value.

I've had horse owners ask me why they should even consider spending over $100 on a handcrafted bit, when they could buy one that looks similar for under $30 from a discount catalog. I'll begin my reply with a couple of analogies.

Have you ever bought a pair of knockoff athletic shoes that looked like Nikes® but were a whole lot cheaper, and that blistered your feet before they quickly fell apart? On the flip side, have you ever owned a pair of western boots so well made that when they finally did need new soles or heels, they were well worth the cost of repair and came back looking and feeling as good as new?

Those scenarios should give you a better understanding of why "cheapest" and "best value" aren't synonymous. When it comes to bits, for example, a horse can feel the difference in what you put in his mouth, just as you can feel the difference in what you put on your feet.

Consider that a bit is a metal device that your horse must carry with the most delicate, sensitive tissues of his body, that his mouth registers taste as well as feel, and that the bit is your primary means of communicating with your horse. You'll gain a whole new appreciation for the kind of bit that isn't stamped out from low-grade materials in a factory overseas.

A handcrafted bit is just that. It's made individually, by hand, by one of the few craftspeople who still practice the bitmaker's art. It'll be balanced and have perfect symmetry between the left side's parts and those on the right, so your horse will feel comfortable carrying it. It'll be made of metals that horses don't find distasteful. The moving parts won't pinch a horse's lips, bars, or tongue. In terms of training, you can get more done with one good bit than you can with a wall full of cheap ones.

Plus, if a handmade bit begins to wear, it can be repaired instead of tossed into a box of junk tack. It'll hold resale value, too, while a low-cost, factory-made bit retains none.

I would rather train and compete in an old saddle made with top-grade materials and workmanship than in a glitzy new one made with corner-cutting materials and processes. I'm sure my horses would agree. To a horse, saddle fit and comfort are everything, while trendy decoration is meaningless. Don't get me wrong, I love a silver saddle as much as anyone does. But if a fancy-looking saddle makes my horse's job harder instead of easier, it's a bad buy at any price.

With horse training, as with carpentry or other crafts, it takes professional-level tools to get professional-level results. If you were to ask me to help you put together a basic tool kit for training performance horses, I'd recommend the following items.

• Ring-style snaffle, $^3/_8$-inch, by Tom Balding, Greg Darnell, Gordon Hayes, Billy Klapper,

or other maker of handcrafted bits. I own scores of bits, but this is my standard, whether training or showing the snaffle-aged horse or fixing an older horse's problems.

• Running martingale, adjustable forks, neck strap, and tie strap, heavy-duty leather, by Cow Horse Equipment or other maker of

success

SUCCESS LESSON

One of my horse-care mentors has been Greg Whalen, a California halter horse breeder and exhibitor I've known for years. Greg takes better care of his horses than anyone else I know—always did, and still does today. Part of what I've learned from him is the value of keeping a horse on a routine, especially when it comes to feeding on a strict time schedule every day. Greg's also a master at reading and feeding his horses as individuals, and spends as much time caring for one after a workout as he does on the workout itself. I've tried to copy that for my own program.

STRAIGHT TRUTH

No matter how talented or well-bred your performance horse, he's nothing if you don't keep him sound.

quality strap goods. The heavier the leather and the more points of adjustability, the more you'll pay—but the martingale will last longer and you can fit various sizes of horses with a single item.

• Nosebands, standard (rests above the bit) and dropped (rests below the bit), same sources as for the martingale. These prevent your horse from getting into the habit of gaping his mouth as he's learning to yield to bit pressure and are as essential to my gear list as a good snaffle.

• Breast collars, single-band and Y-fork, same sources as for other strap goods. No one size or style will fit every horse, so I keep an assortment on hand.

• Split reins, 5/8-inch for snaffles and 1/2-inch for curbs, same strap goods source as earlier. I like the weight of $^5/_8$-inch reins for training and schooling, but want less bulk in my hand for one-handed riding in a curb bit.

• Work saddle, best quality from maker of your choice, fitted to your body build and suited to your horse's activity. For instance, a cutting saddle doesn't give good results when you're training for reining, and vice versa. My favorite saddles are by Donn Leson and Bob's Western Saddles.

• Work pad, engineered for horse's back support, durability, and ease of cleaning. I've tried most that are on the market, and now stick with orthopedic pads by Professional's Choice because they meet all my criteria.

• Protective leg boots, fore and rear, including a set of bell boots. After many years of using them, Professional's Choice products get my nod here too.

(Note: Most of the products mentioned are sold nationwide in major western tack stores.)

• Set of spurs, fitted to your boot-heel size, same sources as for bits. Style is matter of personal choice.

Many aspects of reaching a goal are out of your control, but gear maintenance isn't one of them. By keeping your equipment clean and in good repair, you give yourself one more horsemanship edge.

A horse doesn't care what your tack looks like or what you paid for it. He only knows if it fits him and feels comfortable as you ask him to perform while wearing it. If you compromise on quality, he's the one who has to pay for it.

Feeding Horses

Just remember: *You get out what you put in.*

Anyone who feeds horses has to be concerned about the price of hay, because hay adds up to a big-ticket purchase over a year's time. However, I think it's a mistake to buy your hay supply on the basis of lowest price because this is one category of expense where you definitely get what you pay for. Any grower is going to ask as much for his hay as the area market will bear, and the best hay always brings the best price. A grower wouldn't be offering his hay at a low-end price if it wasn't lacking in some way.

In the long run, cheap, low-quality hay is one of the costliest things you can feed your horses. They'll waste much of it just by picking through the unpalatable portions, so you'll have to feed more volume and dispose of more wastage than you would with better hay. Poor hay won't put bloom on your horses, so if getting that finish is important to your goal, as it would be for a show or resale horse, you'll have to spend more on grain and supplements.

When all's said and done, you'll probably spend more by feeding cheap hay than you saved initially per ton. Plus, you also may find that your horses chew more wood, and I don't have to tell you what that'll do to your buildings, fences, and maintenance costs.

You don't need a degree in agricultural science to become a savvy hay buyer. You should be able to do just fine by using the following tips that have worked well for me.

• Use your network. If you're uncertain about how to recognize quality in a load of hay or don't know where to start looking for it in your neck of the woods, get help from an area horseman whose horses, based on what he feeds, look the way you want yours to look. Ask to see his hay so you can help educate your eye for quality, and find out if he has a hay source you could tap too.

• When you find a supplier whose hay you like, build a good business relationship with him and become a steady customer. I've been buying my hay from the same grower for over 25 years and believe this gives me some clear advantages. I can count on the quality of hay I get and the time of year it'll be delivered. I never have to wonder about the type of ground it's been grown on, or worry about making adjustments for nutritional deficiencies. I don't have to waste time shopping around for hay every time I need a load. My horses also don't have to make big adjustments to their digestive systems each time I start feeding from a new batch.

I'm a big believer in keeping my feed supply "topped off." In other words, I never let my supply of any feedstuff get so low that it's about to run out. I'd rather find another way of controlling my cash flow than to risk an illness-causing interruption in what my horses get fed. This may seem like a minor detail on the track to achieving goals, but it's the neglected minor details that'll derail you every time.

Though I use alfalfa as my horses' primary forage, I also make sure to keep grass hay on hand. Occasionally, I'll get a horse in for training whose digestive system can't tolerate the richness of pure alfalfa. I'll substi-tute part of his hay ration with grass until I find the balance that helps firm up his manure.

The other staples of my feeding program include whole oats, alfalfa pellets, rice bran, loose salt (measured and fed daily in each horse's grain), a vitamin/mineral supplement, corn oil, various nutraceuticals such as MSM and FlexFree, and pelleted daily dewormer. However, I can't give you an exact feeding recipe for these ingredients, because they change periodically. They also vary in mix and proportion from horse to horse.

For instance, I fed a commercial hair-coat supplement for years, but switched to corn oil when the supplement manufacturer

An equine athlete needs excellent nutrition, just as a human athlete does. It's the fuel that runs his performance and rebuilds his body after it's been stressed. Don't cut corners here.

I never let my horses work on a packed, hard surface, because the risk of soundness problems is too great. At my stable we don't start our riding day until the arena's been freshly dragged.

stopped packaging the product in affordable bulk containers. Though I feed whole oats to most of my horses, I don't give it to the ones who get "high" from eating grain. I use the alfalfa pellets to put an extra degree of bloom on the show and futurity horses, but don't want that extra weight on my 2-year-olds in training. Certain horses need to be fed the nutraceuticals in order to stay sound, but others don't.

The majority of my horses get two meals a day, but the real hard keepers get three. My broodmares have hay in front of them at all times, because I want the most timid one in the bunch to get as much to eat as the mares who always get to the feeder first.

Regardless of what you choose to feed your horses, two practices will help you maximize results.

First, eyeball each horse frequently, and feed him as an individual, adding or subtracting feeds as needed to keep him at the weight and condition you want. This is more art than science, and the only way you'll get good at it is by practicing and experimenting. For this reason, I think it helps to do your own feeding rather than turn the job over to someone else.

Second, discipline yourself to feed your horses at the same times every day, even when you have them away from home. Horses thrive on regular mealtimes, and will perform better

for you if they're not worried about their stomachs.

Arena Footing

Just remember: If you don't pay now with regular footing maintenance, you'll pay later with soundness problems.

The subject of arena footing is vast enough to be a book itself. Just like with feeding, there's no single footing recipe that works for every situation and in any locale. However, I can give you the one tip that applies in all cases: The better you maintain the footing you train on, the sounder you can keep your horses.

The cost of regular footing maintenance, in terms of time, labor, and equipment, is greater than many horse people expect. It's something you need to consider before deciding to keep and train your horses at home or to open and operate a public stable. Footing maintenance is an all-too-easy area of management in which to start cutting corners, and an easy chore to put off. Few would argue that it's a lot more enjoyable to be riding horses than to be dragging and watering their training surface.

Unfortunately, your horses will pay for what you save if you let yourself be lax. It doesn't take the proverbial rocket scientist to figure out that compacted ground increases concussion, that rutted tracks can cause hoof-contact injuries, or that having to work in clouds of dust is bad for a horse's lungs. All it takes is one soundness or illness problem at the wrong time, and you can watch your goal pursuit go right up in smoke.

The ideal frequency for dragging an arena is tied directly to frequency and volume of use. The more it's used, the faster its footing will compact and develop ruts, and the more often it'll need to be worked up and smoothed out. At my stable, the arenas are used at least six days a week by over twenty horses, and with that much use, the footing packs down noticeably as a day goes on. I have the ground dragged and refluffed at least once a day, sometimes twice.

Your own "dustometer" will tell you when you need to water your training area. If it's too dusty for you to ride in comfortably, it's too dusty for your horses to be working in. My indoor arena only needs watering every two or three days, but my outdoor arena requires it daily.

Bear in mind that arena footing needs replenishment from time to time; factor that into your maintenance budget and tend to it when necessary. My arenas consist of several inches of sand on top of a packed clay base, and I generally have to add 25 yards of sand to the indoor arena and 100 yards to the outdoor arena every year, to replace dissipated sand or what horses and dragging equipment have tracked out.

Stall Flooring

Just remember: *Surfaces affect soundness.*

Do you have horses who are kept in stalls? If so, what kind of surface are they standing on? Your answer will have a lot to do with how sound you can keep them over time, especially if you're already trying to manage such problems as navicular disease or arthritis.

The vet bill for one leg-contact injury can easily be greater than the price of a set of protective boots. I'm a big believer in their value.

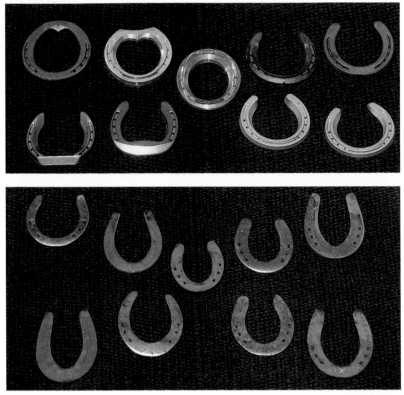

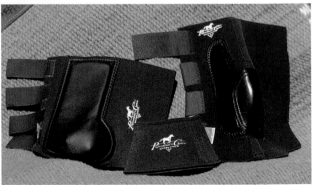

For your best chance at keeping your performance horses sound, pay close attention to what they're wearing from their knees and hocks down. Work with your farrier to find the optimal shoes and shoeing schedule for each horse, and replace your protective legwear as it begins to wear. These shoes are among the various correctives (top left photo) and sliding plates (bottom left photo) in the inventory of my farrier.

A level floor allows a horse to balance his body weight equally over all four legs. That in itself gives him a measure of comfort for the hours he's confined, because he doesn't have to stress one leg for the sake of the other three.

Just imagine how your own body would feel if you had to stand with one foot in a hole and the other on concrete. Then imagine adding hundreds more pounds to the weight being borne, and you'll get some idea of how a horse must feel after supporting himself on a cratered, hard-surfaced stall floor for hours. His body has to pay for it.

Many horsemen testify to the benefits of using rubber mats or other manufactured flooring on top of a leveled stonedust base. Besides being comfortable, this kind of stall surface requires less bedding than bare ground does, and reduces stall-cleaning time.

I wasn't able to afford rubber mats when my barn was built in the 1970s, and other kinds of manufactured stall flooring didn't exist. Wood was relatively cheap at the time, so I opted for a tried-and-true flooring method that dates back to work-horse days; I had my stall floors made of 2 by 8-inch hardwood

diligence

MIND PICTURE

Make soundness come first. Care for your equine athlete as regularly and conscientiously as you would a human sports star whose multimillion-dollar contract gets cancelled if he can't play.

planks installed over a rock drainfield.

This system has its own advantages. The stalls stay level, and the planks don't shift as mats can do. Because urine drains easily instead of pooling on a nonporous surface, the barn's air is free of ammonia, which contributes to respiratory soundness. And, since the planks rest on top of framing beams, they also have a degree of give.

Unfortunately, the increasing scarcity and rising price of wood has made wooden stall flooring cost-prohibitive for most barn owners. If I were going to build a barn now, I'd give serious thought to using mats instead.

People occasionally ask me if I'd put mats over a concrete floor. Though that kind of flooring system would always remain level, I wouldn't use it. Unlike wood or mats over a drainfield, concrete has virtually no give to

it. Even with mats and bedding, it's a harder surface than I'd want my horses to stand on. I've been to some showgrounds with concrete or asphalt stall floors and, no matter how deeply I've bedded them, have ended up with stiff, sore horses by the show's end.

If finances force you to stall your horses on bare dirt, be extra conscientious about filling and leveling holes as they occur. You might suffer some aches and pains from regularly hauling and tamping fill, but you'll reduce them in your horses.

Postride Care

Just remember: The harder you ride a horse, the better you have to take care of him after you pull off the saddle.

If you walked into a pro ball team's locker room after a big game, you'd see that the

trainers' and players' work was far from over. They'd be giving or getting massages, ice treatments, hydrotherapies, and other forms of postplay care and would be putting just as much time and effort into that aspect of their sport as they did in playing the game.

There's a lesson to be learned from the above scenario, which is that any athlete, human or equine, is a living, cellular entity that has to repair itself after it's been physically stressed. The more you aid an athlete in doing this, the better your chances of keeping him sound enough to continue playing.

I'm always telling my assistants, "If you ride a horse really hard one day, you'd better do more than just brush him and put him away. Maybe he needs a body wash, leg bracing, ice wraps, cold-water hosing, anti-inflammatory medication ... it just depends on the individual, and the type of work you did with him. When you've taken a lot out of a horse physically, you need to put just as much back in."

The lack of doing this is one of the biggest problems some riders have, and it seems especially so in the younger generation. They can be so focused on winning and making a name for themselves that they fail to consider the need for hands-on aftercare. They haven't yet learned that there's more to horsemanship than being talented in the saddle. Unfortunately, when they do get the message, it's usually at some poor horse's expense.

Postride care doesn't have to be superscientific in order to be of value. I've used various types of sports-medicine technologies and techniques, from ultrasound to acupuncture, and have found them to be useful in certain circumstances. But when you come right down to it, the simple, old-fashioned horsemanship therapies—ice, cold water, leg braces, body washes, and regular exercise—are still the best, in my opinion.

To me, good aftercare boils down to use of common sense, and to putting yourself in the horse's shoes. If you went out and dug a day's worth of ditches, you know you'd be sore and in need of some physical TLC. You'd want some hot-tub time, a heating pad, an ice pack, a long shower, or whatever else might ease your aches.

If you look at your horses that way, too, you'll be tending to your goals as well as your animals.

details

Seven of My Top Tips for Hair and Hoof Care

If you were to sign on as one of my assistants or as a regular customer, you'd be exposed to the regimen on which I keep my show horses, and would learn I'm very particular about their appearance and their hoof care. These are some key tips you'd see in practice at my barn.

1. Keep your horses very clean. If you don't, dried sweat, manure stains, and ground-in grime will damage their hair. I rinse my horses with warm water after every workout and shampoo and condition their manes and tails once or twice a week. Their stalls are cleaned twice a day, and they're almost always in blankets or sheets for added hair protection.

2. Be proactive with your horses' skin care. You can't have good hair on a horse if he's allowed to have bad skin. At the first inkling of a skin problem, such as ringworm or an itchy mane, I attack it so it doesn't get worse before it gets better. I use a line of antifungal products (Healing Tree developed by Dr. Eric Witherspoon), that includes medicated body wash, shampoo, conditioner, skin cream, and wound spray. I never leave a scratch or abrasion untreated.

3. Care for your horse's mane and tail as though you were caring for your own hair. If you wanted to grow a head of gorgeous, luxurious hair, you'd keep it protected from bad weather, scorching sun, and harsh chemicals. You'd use a quality shampoo. You'd condition the hair regularly, and trim the ends from time to time. The great-hair recipe's no different for a horse.

4. Keep your show horses from getting chilled. A drop in temperature is a trigger for growth of a longer haircoat. My stabled horses wear light sheets almost year-round, but when the barn temperature drops below 65 degrees, I add blankets and hoods. I keep thermometers in the barn and keep the doors of my barn closed on cold, windy days.

5. Clean your saddle pads and horse blankets on a regular basis. Dirty gear harms hair and helps spread skin diseases. My work pads are washed and disinfected every week, and blankets are laundered at least once a month.

6. If a horse's hair quality begins to deteriorate, call your vet. You've probably heard it said that great hair starts from within. Bad hair does, too, and can be the result of any number of systemic problems. Call in your veterinary ally sooner rather than later.

7. Never skimp on farrier care, and keep each horse on a regular, individualized schedule. In much horse literature, you'll find "every six to eight weeks" to be the recommendation for time between shoeings. When it comes to performance horses, that's inadequate. I have my horses reshod every four to six weeks, depending on the individual's rate of hoof growth. You can cause injury to a four-week horse by trying to stretch him to six weeks between resets.

With Your Horse Sense

IF THERE'S any one thing with the power to help you make a big leap toward reaching your horse-related goal, especially if it involves training and competing, it's knowledge of how to work with the equine mind rather than against it.

By knowing what makes sense to horses, you'll gain the kind of horse sense it takes to be fully successful at those activities. Without that knowledge, you'll make errors of approach and judgment that will hold you back, and perhaps even ruin your horse.

I'm basing those statements on the kinds of questions I field regularly from people who are frustrated by roadblocks they're experiencing with their horses. These aren't newcomers to horses as a rule, but people who've been around long enough to have hit a snag and realize they must be missing some key piece of understanding.

These questioners want to know, for instance, why their horses perform perfectly at home but not in the show pen. They want advice on whether to correct unwanted behaviors or ignore them with the hope that they'll go away. They're at their wits' end over mannering their young stallions. They want to know why their horses' performances have gotten worse, not better, over the course of a show season.

I preface my answer to any such question by repeating the old saying that opens this

There's an old saying ...
The horse is a creature of habit.

chapter: The horse is a creature of habit. To me, that's the primary thing you need to remember when practicing your hands-on horsemanship, or when hunting for solutions to training and behavioral problems. In fact, if I've uttered it once, I've probably repeated that statement 10,000 times, as it's the cornerstone of all I do with the horses I train and show.

You'll see what I mean as I delve deeper into this simple but critical aspect of using horse sense to get the most from your horses.

Horse training isn't as complicated as some folks would like to make it. Regular riding and repetition will do more to "make" your horse than most other measures I could name.

success

SUCCESS LESSON

The best way to learn how to discipline a horse who wants to walk all over you is to spend some time observing how horses discipline each other. They begin with a body-language warning sign (a fierce look or a threatening posture) that says, "You'd better get back, or else." If that's ignored, they get physical, usually with one swift, firm, and well-placed connection to a large area of the body. As soon as the offending horse backs off, the other one calmly goes back to minding his own business, without trying to pick a further fight.

Habits, Good and Bad

Worth knowing: *A horse will get good at whatever you allow him to practice.*

If you're like the majority of the goal-driven horse people who come to me for help, you've most likely read every step-by-step, how-to training article you could get your hands on. That's good. It tells me you have a grasp of how horses can be habituated to perform specific skills. Purposeful training is really nothing more than using repetition and reinforcement to instill the habits you want a horse to learn.

What you might not be aware of, however, is the extent to which horses habituate on even the smallest thing, inside the training pen and out. As a creature of habit, the horse is hardwired to detect action patterns, make associations, and form habituated responses. The more times a horse is allowed to repeat and get a benefit from a behavior, desirable to you or not, the faster and more solidly that behavior will become a habit. This is why you need to manage and train your horses not only in ways that deliberately create good habits, but that also prevent inadvertent formation of bad ones.

I'll illustrate this point with four situations and responses taken from my questions file.

Situation 1: An owner is starting her 2-year-old filly under saddle. Whenever she's bridled and ridden, but not at any other times, the filly hangs her tongue out the left side of her mouth. She's been checked by a vet, who found nothing wrong inside her mouth. The owner wants to know if she should change bits, or just ignore the problem and hope it eventually goes away.

My response: Though a different bit might be worth a try, ignoring the problem would be a bad idea. Tongue-hanging is a nervous habit, similar to nail-biting in humans, and only gets more ingrained in a horse who's allowed to continue doing it.

To prevent further reinforcement, I'd ride

such a horse with a dropped noseband fitted snugly enough to keep the tongue inside the mouth. I'd use it every single time I rode, through all the 20 or so months of training I put on a performance horse before he's ever shown, and I'd remove it only when the horse was being judged. I might not get a 100 percent cure for the tongue habit, as it's one of the toughest ones to break. But at least I'd have kept it from getting worse.

(Note: As you can see from many of the photos in this book, I employ some variety of noseband as part of my standard training equipment. I use this gear as a bad-habit preventive. I don't want my horses to ever learn that they can escape bit pressure by gaping at the mouth.)

Situation 2: The owner of a yearling western pleasure prospect has started teaching the horse to longe, and notes that he sometimes crossfires (lopes on the wrong lead with the hind legs) when going to the right. She wonders if she should insist on correcting the horse, or let him lope the way he wants to at this point, and worry about the bad lead later.

My response: Insist on the correct lead right from the start. Otherwise, the horse gets to practice his crossfiring lope, strengthening the muscles that produce this mangled gait and making it easier and easier for him to lope incorrectly as time goes on.

Situation 3: In an effort to help him learn some manners, an owner decides to take my advice and turn his studdy yearling colt out with an older horse. Because he's worried that the colt might get hurt, the owner chooses his kindest, most mild-tempered gelding as a pasture mate. The colt repeatedly mounts and tries to breed the gelding, who is too timid to object. Should the owner leave these two together, he wonders, or put a different horse out with the colt?

My response: Substitute another horse, and pick one that's closer to the top of the pecking order than the bottom. A dominant, cranky old broodmare would be my first choice, because she'd take a no-nonsense approach to making a gentleman out of a colt who doesn't want to be one. By leaving the original pair together, the owner would only give the colt more opportunities to put his raging hormones into action, and to confirm his lack of manners.

Situation 4: A non-pro has trained and schooled her all-around prospect in draw reins in order to keep his head down and his gaits slowed. He works great as long as he's in the draw reins, but when the owner takes them off to show in the required, "legal" reins and bit, she says that "his head's in my face and he gets going so fast that I practically need goggles." She wants to know why this happens, even after her many months of

When I start my young horses by using two hands and a snaffle, my ultimate goal is to be able to ride them one-handed in a curb bit. For that to work, the horses need to learn the meaning of rein pressure on their necks. That's why I keep my hands close together for most snaffle-phase training instead of holding them spread apart, as you see many people do.

schooling in a draw-reins setup.

My response: The extensive draw-reins practice hasn't taught this horse to lower his head and slow down, it's taught him the habit of depending on draw reins for his balance point. As soon as they come off, the horse is lost, because his artificial balancing aid has been removed. Since he hasn't been taught the habit of staying balanced and collected with rein, leg, and seat cues that can be used in the show ring, he has no means for performing up to the owner's expectations.

Tony Amaral always used to say, "If something you're doing with a horse isn't working, don't keep doing it." It's some of the best advice he ever gave me, because it's kept me from giving horses the chance to get good at doing things the wrong way.

Show-Horse Maintenance

Worth knowing: *If you fail to correct show-ring behavior problems where they occur—*

in the show ring—they will only get worse.

Every show horse eventually learns to tell the difference between when he's being shown, and when he's not. That's part of what's behind the very common phenomenon of the horse that works perfectly at home or in the warm-up arena, only to become a cheating son-of-a-gun whenever he's being judged.

People often look at me sideways when I say that horses can tell when they're being shown, as though they're thinking, "Yeah, right—and my horse is smart enough to prepare your taxes." Well, what's smart to us and what's smart to a horse are two different things. The reason horses can tell when

STRAIGHT TRUTH

Every time you handle or ride a horse, you're helping him learn habits. It's up to you to decide whether he learns good habits or bad ones on even the smallest thing.

they're being shown goes right back to their being creatures of habit. As such, they're programmed to seek clues to predictability, and what's more predictable than a horse-show class?

Put yourself into that scene, from a horse's point of view. There's always an announcer and a loudspeaker system, a herd of unfamiliar horses waiting at the arena gate, and a group of people with white squares (their entry numbers) in the middle of their backs. Inside the arena, the horse usually sees a stern-faced person carrying a clipboard, and spectators lining the rail. This set of circumstances

doesn't come together at any other time in the horse's life.

Furthermore, most horses wear specific tack at shows—headstalls, halters, saddles, and so forth—that they don't wear any other time. Their riders dress in identifiable ways too. During warm-up and practice sessions, for instance, it's common for many contestants to be wearing visors or ball caps. But when it's show time, they all wear cowboy hats or hunt caps. A horse takes in about 90 percent of his information from visual input, so believe me, he notices and links these sights to his circumstances.

Once a horse has learned to identify a show-class setting, he can link it with something else that usually happens only in that setting: If his rider or handler is the typical competitor eager to keep a judge's favor, the horse is allowed to get away with things that would be corrected immediately and firmly at any other time. Instead of making an obvious fix that might affect his placing in the class, the exhibitor tries to bluff it out and finish the class with little or no correction.

Unless you're conscious of avoiding this trap, your show horse will make a conclusion that's going to cost you. He'll learn that in this setting, the rules are different, and he can do what he wants. Before long, his transgressions can escalate from minor to major, turning him into one of those chronically

In competition, a reiner always performs his turnarounds at the center of the arena. To reduce show-ring anticipation problems, I do my turnaround training and schooling anywhere but the center of my arena. This helps the horse learn to take his cues from me, not from his location.

cheating, "gotcha" show horses I warned you about in Chapter 3.

You can see examples of this in action at any kind of horse event, from a local playday to a world championship show. It's manifested by the halter or showmanship horse who entertains himself in the show ring by biting at his lead shank or handler as the judge walks around him. It's responsible for runaway reining runs by horses who guide and rate perfectly at all other times. It's why some horsemanship or equitation horses learn they can blow up during their individual pattern work, and why some rope horses figure out that it's okay to buck after leaving the box. Name any kind of bad behavior that occurs only in the show ring, and you'll have evidence of a show-smart horse.

The best way to deal with this sort of problem is to adjust your competitive mindset. Instead of always "riding for the ribbon," focus on keeping your horse correct, listening, and obedient, using the same measures and degree of firmness you do at any other time. By doing this consistently, every time you show, you'll teach your horse that the rules aren't different when he's in a show-ring setting. Even if a show-ring correction costs you a placing, your future performances will be the better for it.

I refer to this mindset and process as "show-horse maintenance." It's also known as "show-pen schooling." Without it, even the most talented performer won't stay good for long.

I frequently enter my horses in show classes not with the intention of winning a prize, but with the plan of fixing, in the show ring, any behaviors the horse might have begun to exhibit there. I'll give you useful examples of show-horse maintenance strategies at the end of this chapter.

revelation

MIND PICTURE

Everything your horse does is a reflection of you and the habits you've either taught him or allowed him to pick up. Step back and ask yourself what these reflections tell people about your handling and training. Then decide if that's what you really want to be said.

Routine Analysis

Worth knowing: The routines you establish have the power to work for you or against you.

As creatures of habit, horses will relax best, learn fastest, and stay healthiest when kept on regular routines. This applies not just to meal times, but also to training schedules, hauling and stabling arrangements, and most other aspects of their lives. It's why I'm such a stickler about maintaining the management routines I've set for my barn. I'm only using Mother Nature to my advantage.

However, because they desire and can identify routines and action patterns, horses also form associations and anticipatory behaviors at the drop of a hat. That can work to your disadvantage. Unless you stop to analyze the full effect of all the routines you employ, using your head to manage them in ways that create the associations you want, you'll set yourself up for problems in your pursuit of success.

Here are five practices from my training program that I've tailored to this principle.

Practice 1: I don't isolate my youngest performance prospects when I begin their training. Instead, I train them from Day 1 in the company of other horses, because that's how they'll be expected to perform for the rest of their lives.

You've probably heard or read that the ideal place for starting a colt is in a solid-sided round pen or other enclosure that keeps out all distractions. I disagree, because it establishes a routine and set of expectations that only have to be erased and replaced at some point down the road.

I do have a round pen on my property, but it's rail-sided and right next to the outdoor arena where older horses are always galloping, sliding, or working cattle. By exposing my young horses to such activities right from the get-go, I'm able to clearly test their reactions and attention span, and work with them accordingly.

Along the same lines, I don't house my flightiest, spookiest young horses in the quietest part of the barn. Instead, I stall them in the busiest part of the barn, so they can learn and adjust to the come-and-go routine of workers, trucks and tractors, and other horses.

Practice 2: Once I've determined that a horse is physically and mentally mature enough to be ridden, I ride him six days a week, even if only for five minutes.

If your goal is to end up with a dependable

performance horse, you won't do him or yourself any favors by keeping him on an erratic riding schedule, or by giving him lots of days off so he can "just relax and be a horse." Horses learn their jobs and accept having to perform them by doing them on a routine basis. When your horse spends more days off during a week than he does under saddle, it only stands to reason that he'll be more inclined to prefer his leisure activities to his work.

Here's another reason for incorporating regular riding into your schedule: Near-daily work gets a horse fit, keeps him that way, and greatly reduces the incidence of training injuries. Compare this to working out at a gym in your own pursuit of fitness. If you were to go only once or twice a week, you'd be stiff and sore on the other days, and wouldn't make much progress. But if you made it a habit to go to the gym almost daily, you'd get fit and stay fit, and be the better athlete for it.

Practice 3: I teach my horses to give me their attention as a matter of routine. If I don't deliberately ask for and recapture their wandering attention at home, I won't have created a habit I can call on later, in competition.

When it comes to attention span, a young horse in training is just like a child going to pre-school. He won't develop the ability to listen attentively to his teacher for any length of time unless the teacher is aware enough to create circumstances that allow him to practice the skill. As I'm riding a horse, I stay alert for signs of wandering attention so I can react immediately and deliberately to regain it.

Let's say I'm riding circles on a colt at the far end of my arena, when another rider opens the gate to bring in his horse. Instead of keeping at least one ear turned back toward me, an indicator of attentiveness to the rider, my colt puts both ears forward to look over at the gate. To recapture his attention, I'll simply cue the colt to speed up or slow down, to change directions, to start another maneuver—anything to remind him that I'm still on his back, and still the one in control. I know I have his attention when he tips at least one ear back toward me.

Practice 4: I teach a horse the routine involved with performing away from home, before expecting to actually show him. To do this, I haul him to a number of shows ("take him to town," as trainers say) for the sole purpose of exposing him to the routine and letting him get used to it.

One reason a young show prospect can perform relatively well at home is that he's become accustomed to his surroundings. He's familiar with the arena, the other horses and people, and the gear and equipment used, and thus develops the habit of working in a known environment.

STRAIGHT TRUTH

A well-broke horse is one who's willing to go right to work, and he gets that attitude from being worked on a regular basis. I've never met a horse yet who taught himself how to work while hanging out in the pasture.

But on his first few trips away from home, thrust into the unfamiliar environment of a competition, a potential show horse has no idea what to expect. His senses will be overloaded by all the comings, goings, and general commotion. Until he gets the comfort of knowing what's going to happen to him after he's unloaded and expected to work in a strange

place, he can't relax enough to give you his full attention.

That's not the state of mind you want a horse to be in when you show him for the first time. As a creature of habit, he'll imprint on the experience, and it's bound to be one that's less than perfect, if not downright bad. The next time you show him, you'll have that negative memory to overcome.

Practice 5: I keep routines and patterns out of my training sessions.

Because horses are so quick to detect, remember, and anticipate anything resembling a pattern, I'm very conscious of putting variety and lack of patterning into my daily training rides. Without a routine to count on, the horse has to pay closer attention to me for his directions on what to do, and that has a show-pen payoff.

For instance, instead of always working a reiner on turnarounds or lead changes at the middle of the arena, where those maneuvers commonly are called for at shows, I'll ask a horse to turn around and change leads everywhere but the middle of my arena. By not giving him a chance at home to link location with maneuver, I prevent a lot of center-pen anticipation problems at shows.

The more thought you put into matters like these, the better you can stay one step ahead of your horse, and the more success you'll have with him.

I teach my colts the meaning of a neck-rein cue almost from the start of their training so that response to neck reining becomes a habit. Once a colt will give his nose to a direct-rein pull, I use direct rein to start him in the new direction, then follow immediately with opposite-side rein and leg pressure to complete the turn. Eventually, those become his only cues.

planning

Show-Horse Maintenance Strategies

When your objective is to establish and maintain good show-ring habits in a horse, you must accept having to sacrifice the occasional paid-for run in order to remind him, on the spot, that you call the shots no matter where he is. Keep in mind that although horses are capable of knowing when they're being shown and when they're not, they can't tell the difference between a major competition with a $500 entry fee and a local schooling show with a $5 entry fee. For your best chances of getting a correct performance when it really matters, precede your big-show run with maintenance outings to smaller, less expensive shows.

- Problem: After being shown a few times, your reiner begins to shut down on turnaround speed before completing his second set of four spins. Maintenance strategy: The next time or two you show him, be ready for him to make the error, and when he does, turn him around several more times instead of letting him quit after the fourth spin.

- Problem: Your rail-event horse learns to listen to the announcer, making his gait changes when he hears the P.A. system click on instead of waiting for you to cue him. Maintenance strategy: Be prepared for gait-change announcements to occur, planning to hold your horse at his present gait even as other horses strike off into the new one. Keep him in the gait you've established for however long it takes him to stop trying to change on his own.

- Problem: In his western-riding classes, your horse begins to anticipate his lead changes down the line of markers, tensing up and attempting to charge into his changes several strides too early. Maintenance strategy: Begin your line of changes on the counter lead, then change from counter lead to counter lead, rather than from normal lead to normal lead. Or, begin on one lead and then insist that your horse stay in that lead, rather than change leads, as he proceeds down the line of markers.

- Problem: While waiting for the steer to leave, your rope horse refuses to stand flat-footed in the box. He leaps through the barrier as soon as he sees the chute operator release the steer. Maintenance strategy: Instead of following the steer as he departs, "score" him by holding your horse back in the box until he's willing to stand. Then walk him out of the box in the direction the steer went.

Superslide '98
Sussex, BC – October 16-17, 1998
$2000 Added Open Derby Champion

Win

by Finding the Right Playing Field

HAVE YOU ever given much thought to the horse industry's levels and niches, and tried to pinpoint where you can have the best fit? If not, you should. You'll help yourself avoid one of the biggest success killers I can name—which is wanting to be something you're not.

Don't get me wrong. I think a person should always strive to be the best he or she can be. But dreams and reach, or dreams and the realistic means to extend reach, don't always match. When you wear boots that don't fit, you won't walk very far before you start to feel them pinch.

Some people take offense at the notion that they and their horses fit into some levels of the industry but not others. I see this is a form of personal barn blindness. That the horse industry stratifies itself isn't a judgmental or moral issue. It's just a fact. You can find analogies almost everywhere else you look.

For example, the automotive industry includes used cars, medium-priced cars, luxury cars, and more. Each level includes people who design cars, sell them, or service them, build them, or dismantle them. Just because a person with an interest in cars doesn't deal at one level of the industry doesn't mean he or she can't enjoy success at another.

Likewise, the horse industry has people who've found ways to be successful with cheap horses, expensive horses, miniature

There's an old saying ...
Everyone has to start somewhere.

horses, supersized horses, and everything in between. Some people find their places at a local level while others find their fits within a broader scope.

No matter where they fit, these people have become winners in their areas of interest by first identifying, then accepting and striving at the levels they find workable. In this chapter are pointers on how you can go about doing the same thing.

Whether you're an old hand at competition or someone who's just starting to learn how to ride, you'll get the most enjoyment from your pursuit of horse world success by matching your goal to your interests, abilities, and resources. These assets are as uniquely yours as your best-fitting boots.

Play Where You Can Pay

Words to win with: *Every goal carries costs, and only you know what you can afford to spend.*

There's no question that every level of horse activity has its costs and tangible rewards, and that both tend to increase the higher you go. This is true of any hobby, sport, or business. For instance, it costs less money to hit golf balls in your backyard

You can't automatically buy your way into success in the horse world, because there's a lot more to it than dollars. No matter how strapped or wealthy you might be, you'll have to pay certain kinds of dues that have nothing to do with writing checks.

than to play in a tournament on the course at Pebble Beach. But beyond personal satisfaction, backyard golfing has less potential payback than the costlier venue too. It's up to you to find the right balance on the scale of costs versus benefits.

A goal's price goes beyond dollars, a fact that people often forget. Along with money, your goal extracts a toll on your time, talents, emotions, relationships, perhaps even your job or career. By failing to take these hidden costs into consideration, you'll face obstacles you didn't even know were coming. Here are some illustrations.

Suppose you enjoy showing or otherwise competing. You've conquered the local level of open competition, and now you'd like to test yourself and your horse at breed shows or regional contests. You've accepted and budgeted for the need to upgrade some of your tack and equipment, and realize you'll probably have to pay more association dues and higher entry fees once you take your step up.

Can you pay? Unless you live in a horse-event hotbed, your new goal will involve more travel and more time away from home. You'll burn vacation time in addition to weekends and long holidays, and may need someone to cover on the home front while you're gone. Your boss, co-workers, and family may come to resent your absences. Because you'll be among the new green pups instead of the old

success

SUCCESS LESSON

When I think of people with the willingness to build on what they have, I think of the woman who had me start the $1,800 colt she'd purchased as a weanling and paid for with $100 monthly installments. Though this horse represented all her hopes and dreams, she let him go for a substantial offer early in his training and used the proceeds for a down payment on her family's first house. She had to start from scratch to finance her next horse, but said, "I did it once, and I can do it again." Three years later, she stood in the winner's circle as the owner of a futurity champion.

top dogs, your ego and emotions may feel beaten up at first by everything from loss of status to an increase in mistakes and failures.

Some people have resources for dealing with such move-up costs, but others don't. If you're in the latter group, you might be more satisfied in the long run by staying at your current level of competition, but challenging yourself with a new horse or event. Or you might need to modify your move-up mission in some other way that's a better match for your personality and personal setting.

Here's another common situation. Picture yourself as someone who'd rather step back from the travel-oriented pace of arena competition in order to raise performance prospects and subsequently spend more horse time at home. You figure you can buy a lot of stud-fee power for what you used to spend on the show circuit and besides, you're ready for a break.

Can you pay? Without the built-in travel and trend-exposure time, you'll have to make a concerted effort to keep up with what's happening in the market you'll be breeding

for. You'll be switching from competitor to maternity caretaker and reproduction manager, which requires a completely different set of horsemanship skills that some folks find very anxiety-producing. Once your foals are on the ground, you'll have to become part

Learning a new sport comes with costs that go beyond the price of lessons. You also pay with patience, mistakes, and the occasional bruising of your ego. If you can handle the hidden tolls, you'll make progress.

STRAIGHT TRUTH

Every dream has limits. Compare winning in the horse world to winning at basketball. You can fantasize all you want about playing alongside someone of Michael Jordan's caliber. But if you're stuck with a height of 5 feet, 6 inches, and you still want to be successful in basketball, you need to look somewhere other than the NBA court to find your place.

trainer, part marketing expert, part sales vendor. In the meantime, the demands on your other horsekeeping resources, including feed and space, will increase each time you raise a new crop without having sold the previous one.

Know what will greet you before you decide to go there because the breeding side of the

If what you're doing isn't fun, I firmly believe you should be doing something else. I think we each have to take as much responsibility for our own fun, however that's defined, as we do for our own success.

horse industry might not be for you. Perhaps you'd be better suited to another home-based horse pursuit, such as buying yearlings and conditioning them for resale or boarding horses who are on rehabs or layoffs.

I'll give you one more example of a common goal and its not-so-obvious costs. Say you decide to pursue a career as a professional trainer. You've taken all the steps I recommend, from getting early horse experience and post-high school education to serving an apprenticeship with an established pro. You've rented a barn and will be on your own with a list of prospective clients who have quality horses.

Can you pay? As anyone who's ever done it can tell you, being your own boss requires its own brand of discipline. You have to figure out how to maximize the riding hours in your day, because you also have to run the place, deal with customers, field phone calls and other inquiries, and so forth. Besides earning your money, you have to bill for it, collect it, and keep track of its outgo. If you slack off, the cash-flow demands of the training business will eat you alive. Also realize that you pay your own medical and disability insurance and your own Social Security tax. You have to save and plan for your own retirement too.

If all that sounds like too big a pain, perhaps you're better suited to being a trainer

Finding ways to satisfy the urge to learn has become a huge trend that began with the 1990s countdown to the new millennium. The changeover to the 2000s activated something in human nature that's boosted our desire to learn more, as a way to avoid being left behind. I don't foresee an end to this trend anytime soon.

I'm sure we've all known horse people who spend a good amount of energy complaining how their lack of resources holds them back from reaching their goals. They talk a lot about their "don't-haves." They don't have enough time, don't have enough money, don't have the horse, don't have the right facilities, don't have the ideal location, don't have the trainer, don't have the market, don't have this, that, or the other. They often take their don't-haves personally, as though "the system" were conspiring against them to keep them from being successful.

When I hear this sort of talk from someone, my first thought is, "Your problem isn't about lack of resources, it's about having a goal that's inappropriate for the resources you do have." To be reachable, any goal has to be built on the foundation of current resources and personal reality. You can't climb higher by stepping into thin air.

Successful goal-seekers take the measure of their resources, however meager, then craft stepping-stone goals with those. Even if all they can manage is the tiniest bit of progress, they're already ahead of the complaining don't-havers who fail to take this approach. I'll give you success-building examples based on real-life situations of horse people I've worked with.

Let's say you're an aspiring small-scale breeder of performance prospects. Your assets

who's employed by someone than to running your own business. The employed-trainer option leaves most of the paperwork and cash-flow headaches to someone else. Or, your best fit could be to have a steady nonhorse job with good benefits and to train horses on the side.

Don't Get Mad, Get Real

Words to win with: *You're better off acknowledging and leveraging what you do have than lamenting what you don't.*

STRAIGHT TRUTH

When you possess a goal, you're the one who's responsible for it. No one else can reach it for you, or step in to do your learning for you. You are the one in charge.

include two young broodmares with excellent pedigrees and their first yearlings, who are by well-known performance stallions. However, the mares lack performance records of their own, and now that you've got your money tied up in the mares and the expense of stud fees, you don't have the means to get those first offspring trained and campaigned. How do you build on your reality after learning about the marketplace's demand for dam-side credentials in prospects?

Do-have strategy: Enhance your mares' credentials by giving a whole or part interest in their yearlings to someone who does have a way to get those first offspring trained and campaigned to some sort of achievement level. It could be a professional who doesn't have to pay out-of-pocket for training or a non-pro who can afford monthly training and show fees but not the full purchase price of a prospect.

Though you won't pocket as much money on the yearlings as you might have wanted, you'll have taken a step toward making your mares' future offspring more appealing and therefore more valuable.

If you don't take that step, you may find yourself having to unload the yearlings at a slashed price to the first person who comes along, just to make room for your mares' next foals. The first foals won't do your broodmares any good if they disappear into some bargain hunter's back pasture.

In another scenario, let's say you're a non-pro rider who'd like to get into the sport of reining. Your assets include a good job, good credit, and a gelding you show in rail events. However, your current horse doesn't have the talent or training to be a reiner, and the money you could get for him isn't enough to buy a trained reining horse at today's prices. Where can you go from here?

Do-have strategy: Make friends with the concept of delayed gratification. Sell your present horse and bank the proceeds. Then, for the next year or however long it takes, add to that new-horse seed money by disciplining yourself to set aside what you'd have spent on the old horse's upkeep, vet bills, tack, show fees, etc. Since you won't have a horse taking up your free time for a while, you may be able to take on some overtime hours or outside jobs as a way to beef up your bankroll.

If the total of your savings still won't get you into a good first reiner, consider adding to it with funds from a line of credit. People buy other kinds of vehicles this way, and while I'm not advising you to mortgage the farm in order to buy a horse, a small loan could be what it takes for you to top off your new-horse fund. Loan or no loan, you'll be much closer to your goal of getting into reining after your year off than you'd be if you sat back and did nothing to change your status quo.

My wife, Christy, is fond of saying, "If you can't reach your goal, change it." I think that's another way of expressing the fact that reachable goals must be adjusted to match resources.

Though my success depends on a steady supply of high-quality performance prospects, I'd rather train and show horses than run a breeding farm. I leave that to people who are just as passionate about their chosen aspect of industry involvement as I am about mine.

Seek Satisfaction

Words to win with: *If you're doing something that isn't satisfying, you should look at doing something different.*

We all have our reasons for what we pursue and do with horses and our own versions of what constitutes a rewarding outcome. When you are struggling to keep going, even after using your resources for all they're worth, your internal monitor is trying to tell you something. You're shopping for success at a "reward store" that doesn't carry what you want most.

What do you want as the primary outcome of your goal? In my case, I want to excel and be considered among the best at what I do. But other goal-seekers want to acquire or pos-

sess something, such as money or a specific quality of horse. Others want the reward of being able to say, "I made something from nothing," or, "I did this on my own."

Some people get their chief satisfaction from serving or helping others, but others are geared toward gaining attention or recognition for themselves. I've known horse people whose main source of satisfaction comes from being an anonymous member of a team and others who aren't happy unless they can be the leaders of their packs.

More chief rewards for certain individuals include security, self-improvement, athletic mastery, influencing others, "fixing" or rescuing horses with problems, or being pioneers in unexplored fields. Some people get the biggest kick out of being able to say, "I beat the 'big boys,'" or from doing "what couldn't be done." Some are motivated by fitting in, but others have their bells rung by standing out and being different.

Before you do any further work toward your horse goal, examine it from this perspective. Ask yourself, "What is the one outcome I want most, and can this goal reasonably provide it?" When the answer to the second part of that question is "no," you need to make some kind of change or shift. Otherwise, you'll be on a path toward frustration instead of on the path to reaching your goal.

realism

MIND PICTURE

If your resources won't allow you to play at the high level of your dreams, play at a lower level, and work to become its star. When you've succeeded at that, the next level's door will open for you automatically in ways you never expected. Excellence always attracts opportunities.

Most people tend to resist change because it means letting go of what's familiar and stepping out into the unknown. This is a normal part of human nature, whether it involves horses or not. When something is predictable, even if it's negative, frustrating, or otherwise dissatisfying, it gives a sense of control. I'm sure that's a big reason why people hang onto horses who aren't working out, why they stay home instead of going to clinics and seminars that might help them advance, and why they don't change breeds, barns, levels, or disciplines, even when their gut tells them they should.

But, as someone once told me, "If you don't change something, nothing will change." Sometimes a person's biggest success can be measured not by the end result, but by the beginning act. It doesn't take as much courage to reach the ground in a parachute jump as it does to push yourself out the open airplane door.

When you do decide to make a change, I think it's important to think in terms of what you'll be gaining, not what you'll be giving up. Previous learning doesn't go away just because you'll be doing something that lets you learn more.

I've always thought that change makes a better friend than it does an enemy. If you are willing to adopt that attitude, you'll always be a winner in my book.

A person has to have some success along the way toward a goal, even when just starting out. That's one reason why it's important to think in terms of building on what you do have instead of worrying about what you don't.

25 More Revealing Questions

The more you can create self-savvy, the better your chances of knowing your playing field when you see it. Use your answers to these questions as readily employable assets; by looking to discovery instead of to denial, you'll be on the road to success.

1. What's your primary horse-related interest?

2. How does that translate to your current goal?

3. In terms of the outcome you most want, how do you describe success?

4. If you aren't getting that outcome now, why not?

5. What's your present level of equine involvement?

6. If you're in the horse business, what's your marketplace?

7. What other horse world activities and levels have you experienced?

8. What's the primary lesson you learned from each?

9. What do you value most dearly in life?

10. What about your goal enhances or detracts from that?

11. What have been your greatest successes so far?

12. What resources did you use to achieve them?

13. Which of those resources are still available?

14. How could you put them to use again?

15. Who's your primary contact or mentor in each area of your equine experience?

16. How could those persons assist you in the future?

17. What could you give back in return?

18. What would you rather work with: horses, people, material goods, or ideas?

19. How might your answer affect your current goal?

20. How could you modify your goal, if necessary?

21. What step could you take today to get started?

22. How will you know when your goal has been reached?

23. To whom could you give a hand after each step of your success?

24. How else could you give part of your success back to the horse industry?

25. Where else might that take you?

When you do get your measure of success in the horse world, remember to pass part of it along to someone else. The next generation of horsemen and horsewomen, no matter what the age (this is BJ Avila, Christy's and my son), will grow from what we each plant.

PROFILE: BOB AVILA

IF PEDIGREE and environment contribute as much to a person's destiny as they do to a horse's, it'd be safe to say that Bob Avila had both on his side in becoming a premier professional horseman.

Born in 1951 in Half Moon Bay, Calif., the future world champion was the only child of Don Avila, a former rodeo cowboy turned professional horse trainer, and Pat Avila (now Pat Berry), an avid horsewoman who worked at a western store and modeled western clothing on the side. Don and Pat raised their son in the heart of the West Coast show circuit, in an era when its vaquero-influenced western trainers and their horses set the standard by which others elsewhere were measured.

According to Bob, who began showing well before his teens, his childhood idols were trainers Don Dodge, Tony Amaral Sr., Harry Rose Sr., Clyde Kennedy, and Jimmy Williams. At the heights of their careers during the 1950s and '60s, these winning Californians influenced bloodlines, tack, riding styles, and presentation methods in ways still apparent today.

"I'm sure a lot of other kids looked up to those horsemen, too," says Bob, "but thanks to my parents' involvement with horses, I didn't have to admire them from afar. I was around them almost constantly, at all the shows we went to. They helped raise me."

Bob acknowledges the advantage he got from this exposure.

"I realize how lucky I was to have had those great horsemen as direct influences so early in my life. I know I absorbed things from each one, starting at a very young age, that otherwise would have taken half a lifetime to learn," he states.

"Plus, they were truly horsemen. There was no such thing as specialization in their day. To survive as a trainer, you had to be able to train anything and everything, and they could. To this day, I enjoy producing a good all-around horse, and that comes partly from the influence of my childhood heroes."

The Mentor of Mentors

Amaral, renowned for his ability to spot potential in people as well as horses, would end up being the most influential of Bob's early heroes, even before hiring him as an apprentice trainer and assistant in 1971.

"I was a pretty wild kid," Bob admits. "I absolutely hated high school. I hated it so bad I'd made up my mind to quit, and my parents couldn't talk me out of it. I went to stay with Tony—I'd worked for him during summer vacations—and he talked me into going back to school. I did finish, barely, and I owe that to him.

"I hate to think where I'd be today if I hadn't listened to him," he continues. "Tony didn't

Great horsemen and great horses have been this professional's biggest influences.

In 1999, riding Matt Day's Smart Zanolena, Bob joined the elite group of horsemen who've won the NRCHA World Championship Snaffle Bit Futurity more than once. His previous win was in 1988, aboard Dave Roberts' Smart Little Calboy.

tell me anything all that different from what my parents had tried to tell me, but you know how some kids are. Their parents are the last persons they're going to listen to."

After tasting career success as a highly paid but office-bound salesman of auto parts, and deciding that wasn't the life for him, Bob returned to horses by asking Amaral for a job. The older horseman took him on. In exchange for a place to live and a few hundred dollars a month, Bob rode colts, cleaned stalls, doctored cattle, drove rigs to and from shows, and whatever else the boss needed done, all day long, six days a week. Then, as now, being a trainer's assistant was decidedly unglamorous work.

However, working for this trainer came with a bonus. Like Bob is today, Amaral was known as a trainer's trainer, someone who, by example, could teach young hands how to run a successful business as well as how to train horses. Part role model and part dictator, Amaral insisted on professionalism at every turn, and was as demanding of his help as he was of himself.

"Tony was the person who proved to me the value of hard work," Bob recounts. "Not that I didn't learn something about hard work from my dad, because he was and still is an incredibly hard worker. It's just that with Tony, you didn't whine about working. You did things his way, when he wanted them done, and that was it."

Bob credits Amaral as his biggest influence in other ways.

"From Tony, I learned how to deal with customers, how to spot talent in a horse, how to put a horse deal together, how to hire and fire help, and a million other things I still use every day. He was totally professional in everything he did, and I saw how people respected him for it. He made me want to be just like him," says the former Amaral protégé.

On His Own

By the time Amaral passed away in 1998 at age 72, Bob was well established as a professional horseman. Yet he says he has no trouble in still being able to identify with the young trainers who struggle to establish themselves in their post-apprenticeship businesses. His own first years as a self-employed trainer were lean.

"When I first went out on my own in Oregon, I nearly starved to death," he says. "Just like I do today, I would send horses home that I didn't think were going to live up to their owners' expectations. I've never believed it's fair to keep taking a customer's money for training a horse who lacks ability to progress beyond a certain point.

"But every time I did that," he continues, "I was sending away my income. I usually

FALLAW

Bob got an early taste of reputation-building success in 1974, by winning the open reining at the Cow Palace on Chugwater, "one of my first show horses that I produced as a trainer out on my own." After that, he says, more owners of outstanding horses began to contact him about training.

Bob Chex (left), a working cow horse, was Bob's first national high-point winner, circa 1975. Sparky Girl (below, with Christy Avila) was Bob and Christy's initial ticket to AQHA World Show success when she earned top-ten placings in halter and performance in 1977. Rey Jay Jr. (opposite page), one of Bob's many all-around performers from the 1970s and 1980s, was a winner at cutting, reining, western pleasure, trail, western riding, working cow horse, and halter.

had to ride my bike from my apartment to the barn I was renting, because I wasn't making enough to buy gas for my truck. An instant success, I was not."

In 1974, after agreeing to drive someone else's rig from Portland to San Francisco in exchange for a trailer slot for his lone show horse, Bob got what he considers his first big break. Not quite 23, he won the open reining at the Cow Palace's Grand National, on a nondescript gelding named Chugwater.

"Chugwater was one of my first show horses that I produced as a trainer out on my own," says Bob. "When he won the Cow Palace, he made people notice me. I started to get better horses to train after that. Chugwater was just a little chestnut gelding, but

he gave me a big jack up."

Bob earned his first American Quarter Horse Association national title in 1975, campaigning Bob Chex to the top of the year-end working cow horse standings. He repeated the feat in 1976, this time with Ima Dee Bar, and showed the reserve national high-point winner as well.

That same year, Bob married Christy Skuzeski, the former Quarter Horse youth

competitor he'd been dating for some time. She joined him in his fledgling training business.

Her grandfather, C.F. "Sport" Laughlin, provided the newlyweds with a home base for their horses. Laughlin, who had a passion for raising and showing Quarter Horses, owned an enormous barn and indoor arena complex near Yamhill, Oregon, and gave the couple stall space in exchange for doing work for him. Eventually, he sold them a parcel of nearby land, where they built their present home and training facility.

The Avilas emerged as blue-ribbon regulars on the West Coast Quarter Horse circuit, hauling youth and open horses, and "one or two other horses for Grandpa," as Christy recalls. One of those was the spectacular halter and performance mare, Sparky Girl. Laughlin-bred, she earned top-ten placings in halter and western riding at the 1977 AQHA

World Show, and had four AQHA Superior-Event awards to her credit by the time she was retired.

When Laughlin dispersed his horses for health reasons in the 1980s, Sparky Girl wasn't included. Instead, she was given to Christy, who made sure she lived out her life as the pampered queen of Avila Stables.

"Sparky Girl was one of the last, true, world-class all-around horses," remarks Bob in a tribute to the mare. "She could win the mare grand championship at halter in the morning, and then go out and win all her performance classes in the afternoon. She was the dream horse of a lifetime. In today's market, she'd have been a $1 million mare."

The Major Bonanza Dynasty

One of Bob's favorite sayings is that "it takes great horses to make a great trainer." He would know. His association with Major Bonanza, a superb halter horse who became a superb performer, then a leading sire, finally a significant broodmare sire, propelled both parties to prominence.

Major Bonanza was one of the horses Bob got to train as a result of Chugwater's 1974 reining win at the Cow Palace. Owned by Andy and Carol Rees (who later sold a half interest to Gordy MacDonald), the stallion was a green-broke 3-year-old who had been

winning big at halter since his yearling season.

After several months of further training by Bob, Major Bonanza made his performance debut as an all-around horse. The Avilas showed him in everything from western and English pleasure to cutting and working cow horse, and he was good at all of it. He finished 1977 as AQHA's high-point working cow horse stallion, giving Bob a three-year string of national honors in the event while generating stud-service bookings not just from owners of halter mares, but of performance mares as well.

The Avila-Major Bonanza alliance went to a new level in 1981, when Bob captured his first AQHA World Show title by winning junior cutting on one of the stallion's sons, Major Investment. Major Investment also was reserve champion in junior reining, and third in junior western pleasure.

"He definitely got noticed," says Bob of the impact made by Major Investment's multiple talents.

The next year, Bob repeated his World Show junior cutting win, this time on a Major Bonanza son named The Major Leaguer. With get of this caliber, Major Bonanza was on his way to AQHA leading-sire status, a position he held for nearly a decade while providing Bob and other horsemen with a steady stream of talented prospects and winning performers. Though Major Bonanza passed away in 1998,

When Bob teamed up with Major Bonanza, the careers of both zoomed to "fast forward." Initially a winning halter horse, Major Bonanza became an outstanding all-around horse and sired AQHA world champions (including Bob's first two) in a variety of performance events. His daughters now are well regarded as broodmares.

Bob's list of AQHA world champions includes (this page, top to bottom) The Major Leaguer, Smoke Um Okie, and Major Investment. Smoke Um Okie was the AQHA World Show's Superhorse in 1986. The trainer has also helped launch the flourishing careers of several former assistants, such as John Slack and Todd Bergen (opposite page).

his influence still can be found in Bob's program, as he's now competing and winning on the offspring of Major Bonanza daughters.

"In my opinion, Major Bonanza was largely responsible for adding the 'pretty' factor to today's performance horses," Bob maintains. "Major was a very pretty horse himself, and he passed that on. Before his time, most performance horses weren't necessarily horses you'd look at twice. Major's offspring changed that."

Victories, Additions, and Losses

Bob's star continued to climb during the 1980s, as his training stable continued to deliver a series of world, national, and regional winners on a spectrum from halter to nearly every western performance event. Despite a growing trend toward specialization, not just by horses but by trainers as well, he held fast to the concept of versatility, insisting that "doing the same thing all the time would bore me to death."

As the Avila Stables reputation grew, so did the Avila family, with the birth of son BJ (shortened from Robert Joseph) in 1983. As Bob was, he's being raised as a horseman. BJ's childhood growth changes, going back to when he was still little enough to fit in the saddle with his dad, are recorded in the year-

DON TROUT

by-year framed win photos that line the walls of Bob and Christy's barn.

Bob can name a long list of horses that stand out in his mind from the 1980s, but a sentimental favorite is Smoke Um Okie, the plain bay gelding that he and J.D. Yates showed to win the 1986 AQHA World Show Superhorse honor. Also known as "George" and originally selected by Bob as an amateur mount for owner Kim Fritz, Smoke Um Okie was a regular member of the Avila Stables show string for five years prior to his Superhorse win and

"We had George around here for years after he was retired," Bob continues, "and he was just as great at being a using and teaching horse as he was at being a show horse. BJ learned how to ride and rope on him. He taught most of my non-pros of that era how to change leads, stop, and turn around. We doctored cattle with him, we ponied colts on him—every job you can think of. If you wanted to classify him, Smoke Um Okie was 'America's horse,' the kind of horse everyone dreams of having."

As his most unforgettable accomplishment of the 1980s ("of all time, actually"), Bob names winning the National Reined Cow Horse Association's World Championship Snaffle Bit Futurity. He hit that milestone in 1988 with Smart Little Calboy, after being reserve champion in '86 on Docs Missy Command.

"To me," says Bob, "the Snaffle Bit Futurity is the ultimate challenge, because it requires you to train and show a cutter, a reiner, and a working cow horse, all with one horse. There's a fair number of people who can train a horse for the three events, but not very many who can get a horse shown well enough in all three to make it into the finals, let alone come out on top."

Part of what made the '88 Snaffle Bit Futurity victory so memorable for Bob is that it occurred with his idol, Tony Amaral, in the stands and first in line to shake his hand. But

subsequent retirement from competition. His last set of show shoes, plated and engraved, have a place of honor on a wall.

"Smoke Um Okie was a great horse," Bob states flatly. "I'm not going to say he was the best reiner I ever had, or the best cow horse, or whatever—but he defined greatness as far as I'm concerned. He would never give up. He had times when he could be tough to train, and times when he'd get mad, but even those few times when he didn't want to be good, he would just keep going and going.

he regrets that he didn't get to savor the achievement with two of his other closest friends and mentors, Ben Scott and Bruce Gilchrist. Only in their 40s, both had died earlier in the year, with Scott succumbing to cancer and Gilchrist suffering a fatal heart attack at a show, just minutes after making a winning reining run.

"It would have meant a lot to me to have been able to share that with them," Bob muses. "All the success we were having was great, but it was balanced out by losing such good friends at such young ages."

It was Scott, he says, who'd helped him to view the horse world as an industry, with the same unwritten rules for marketing, merchandising, promotion, and customer service as any other industry.

WALTENBERRY

When Bob won the 1988 NRCHA Snaffle Bit Futurity on Smart Little Calboy (opposite page), his mentor, Tony Amaral, was on hand to congratulate him. Bob won the 1994 National Reining Horse Association Futurity on Lenas Wright On (this page, top), a horse produced from the breeding program he'd set up for owner Jim Wright. Bob's belief that great horses have great mothers is evidenced by the stallion's dam, Slide Me Again; she was runner-up for the AQHA reserve champion Superhorse title one year. Riding Lean With Me (this page, bottom) for owners Jon and Norma Sather, Bob captured AQHA world titles in reining and working cow horse during the 1990s.

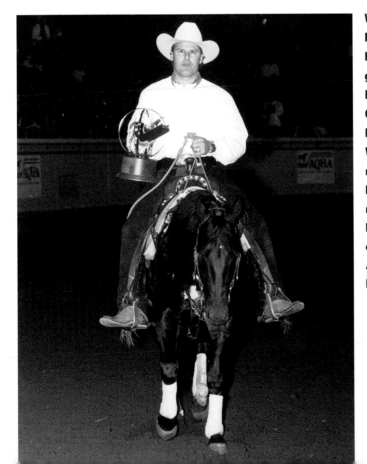

"Ben had the ability to take what he'd learned from being successful in the real-estate business, and apply it to being successful in the horse business," Bob explains.

"As for Bruce, he was my biggest supporter. He also was a misunderstood person who lived in that creative zone between genius and insanity. Some of his ideas about training could get pretty far off the wall, but he had an endless supply of them. He's the person who taught me to think my way through training problems instead of trying to conquer them with emotion and physical strength."

"Never Stop Striving"

While some trainers might have kicked back and cruised after winning their life's-dream event, Bob didn't. Instead, he began looking beyond the familiar world of horses for lessons in how to parlay his trainer/showman reputation into a further franchise. As his guide, he used many of the success-based principles outlined in this book.

By the time the new millennium rolled around, Bob wasn't just training, selling, and showing horses. He'd also developed Heroes & Friends, a line of symposiums and educa-

As Bob's renown as a professional horseman has grown, his training clientele has come from around the world as well as from just down the road. World champion rope horse Chex In My Pocket (this page) was campaigned for owner Hidenubu Kaibara of Japan, while world champion halter gelding Runnin Late (opposite page) added to the trophy collection of Bob's neighbor, Chatty Eliason.

HAROLD CAMPTON

tional videos; partnered with Avila's Pro Shop, a retailer selling high-quality tack and equipment; become identified with a battery of stallions promoted extensively as How The West Was Won; added his name and stamp of expertise to *Ride With Bob Avila*, a monthly horsemanship-focused newsletter and its website, www.ride-withbob.com; and been signed to endorse a variety of horse-related products.

Above all, he'd realized that success with horses can be found in more than one dimension.

"At one time, I thought the only thing I had to do to become successful was to be a winner on horses I'd trained," Bob reveals. "Then I started looking around at other industries, like professional athletics, and saw there could be more to a horseman's pursuits than the ability to play the game."

As a latter-day mentor, Bob cites Matt Day, an Avila Stables customer with a successful

business outside of horses.

"Matt and I don't necessarily always talk about horses," says Bob. "I've learned a lot from him just by being around him, and observing how he handles himself in his regular world. He's helped me learn how to open some new doors."

Still, Bob's continued prowess as a competing pro is what set him apart in the league of horsemen who became brand names in the 1990s.

Examples: Avila-schooled horses or riders won the National Reining Horse Association's open futurity championship or reserve in seven of the decade's 10 years. Bob won the top prize himself in '94, on a horse produced from the breeding program he'd set up for longtime customer Jim Wright. Between 1994 and 1998, Bob and four of his former assistants claimed $1.1 million in reining prize money, approximately one-fifth of the total available in the entire sport at the time.

By the close of the 1990s, Bob had pushed his string of AQHA World Show titles past the 30 mark, won more AQHA year-end high-point titles than he can name off the top of his head, captured the NRCHA Snaffle Bit

DON TROUT

As is true for both his parents, BJ Avila has been familiar with the inside of a show arena from a very young age. He's gone from being a leadline contestant (far left) to a two-time AQHA youth world champion, winning top titles in reining and team roping, heeling. In this photo, he's heading for his dad.

Futurity crown a second time, and shown 1999's leading reined cow horse money earner. He'd even helped extend the line of Avila world champions to the next human generation, by coaching son BJ to win the reining class at the 1997 American Youth Quarter Horse Association World Championships.

Bob kicked off 2000 by winning the NRCHA's World's Greatest Horseman title and saw his son win the AYQHA world championship in team roping, heeling, and the reserve world championship in team roping, heading.

It's BJ, says Bob, who's his biggest present-day mentor and guiding light to the next professional avenues he'll explore, whatever they might turn out to be.

"Being around BJ, and watching him learn and progress as a horseman in today's world, is inspiring me to keep looking toward the future. He helps me stay young in my thinking, and is my reminder that what's worth knowing is worth passing on."

—Juli S. Thorson

The *Western Horseman*, established in 1936, is the world's leading horse publication.
For subscription information: 800-877-5278. To order other *Western Horseman* books: 800-874-6774.
Western Horseman, Box 7980, Colorado Springs, CO 80933-7980. Web-site: www.westernhorseman.com.

Books Published by Western Horseman Inc.

ARABIAN LEGENDS by Marian K. Carpenter
280 pages and 319 photographs. Abu Farwa, *Aladdinn, *Ansata Ibn Halima, *Bask, Bay-Abi, Bay El Bey, Bint Sahara, Fadjur, Ferzon, Indraff, Khemosabi, *Morafic, *Muscat, *Naborr, *Padron, *Raffles, *Raseyn, *Sakr, Samtyr, *Sanacht, *Serafix, Skorage, *Witez II, Xenophonn.

BACON & BEANS by Stella Hughes
144 pages and 200-plus recipes for delicious western chow.

BARREL RACING by Sharon Camarillo
144 pages and 200 photographs. Tells how to train and compete successfully.

CALF ROPING by Roy Cooper
144 pages and 280 photographs covering roping and tying.

CUTTING by Leon Harrel
144 pages and 200 photographs. Complete guide on this popular sport.

FIRST HORSE by Fran Devereux Smith
176 pages, 160 black-and-white photos, about 40 illustrations. Step-by-step information for the first-time horse owner and/or novice rider.

HEALTH PROBLEMS by Robert M. Miller, D.V.M.
144 pages on management, illness and injuries, lameness, mares and foals, and more.

HORSEMAN'S SCRAPBOOK by Randy Steffen
144 pages and 250 illustrations. A collection of handy hints.

IMPRINT TRAINING by Robert M. Miller, D.V.M.
144 pages and 250 photographs. Learn to "program" newborn foals.

LEGENDS by Diane C. Simmons
168 pages and 214 photographs. Barbra B, Bert, Chicaro Bill, Cowboy P-12, Depth Charge (TB), Doc Bar, Go Man Go, Hard Twist, Hollywood Gold, Joe Hancock, Joe Reed P-3, Joe Reed II, King P-234, King Fritz, Leo, Peppy, Plaudit, Poco Bueno, Poco Tivio, Queenie, Quick M Silver, Shue Fly, Star Duster, Three Bars (TB), Top Deck (TB), and Wimpy P-1.

LEGENDS 2 by Jim Goodhue, Frank Holmes, Phil Livingston, Diane C. Simmons
192 pages and 224 photographs. Clabber, Driftwood, Easy Jet, Grey Badger II, Jessie James, Jet Deck, Joe Bailey P-4 (Gonzales), Joe Bailey (Weatherford), King's Pistol, Lena's Bar, Lightning Bar, Lucky Blanton, Midnight, Midnight Jr, Moon Deck, My Texas Dandy, Oklahoma Star, Oklahoma Star Jr., Peter McCue, Rocket Bar (TB), Skipper W, Sugar Bars, and Traveler.

LEGENDS 3 by Jim Goodhue, Frank Holmes, Diane Ciarloni, Kim Guenther, Larry Thornton, Betsy Lynch
208 pages and 196 photographs. Flying Bob, Hollywood Jac 86, Jackstraw (TB), Maddon's Bright Eyes, Mr Gun Smoke, Old Sorrel, Piggin String (TB), Poco Lena, Poco Pine, Poco Dell, Question Mark, Quo Vadis, Royal King, Showdown, Steel Dust, and Two Eyed Jack.

LEGENDS 4
Several authors chronicle the great Quarter Horses Zantanon, Ed Echols, Zan Parr Bar, Blondy's Dude, Diamonds Sparkle, Woven Web/Miss Princess, Miss Bank, Rebel Cause, Tonto Bars Hank, Harlan, Lady Bug's Moon, Dash For Cash, Vandy, Impressive, Fillinic, Zippo Pine Bar, and Doc O' Lena.

PROBLEM-SOLVING by Marty Marten
248 pages and over 250 photos and illustrations. How to develop a willing partnership between horse and human to handle trailer-loading, hard-to-catch, barn-sour, spooking, water-crossing, herd-bound, and pull-back problems.

NATURAL HORSE-MAN-SHIP by Pat Parelli
224 pages and 275 photographs. Parelli's six keys to a natural horse-human relationship.

REINING, Completely Revised by Al Dunning
216 pages and over 300 photographs showing how to train horses for this exciting event.

ROOFS AND RAILS by Gavin Ehringer
144 pages, 128 black-and-white photographs plus drawings, charts, and floor plans. How to plan and build your ideal horse facility.

STARTING COLTS by Mike Kevil
168 pages and 400 photographs. Step-by-step process in starting colts.

THE HANK WIESCAMP STORY by Frank Holmes
208 pages and over 260 photographs. The biography of the legendary breeder of Quarter Horses, Appaloosas, and Paints.

TEAM PENNING by Phil Livingston
144 pages and 200 photographs. How to compete in this popular family sport.

TEAM ROPING WITH JAKE AND CLAY by Fran Devereux Smith
224 pages and over 200 photographs and illustrations. Learn about fast times from champions Jake Barnes and Clay O'Brien Cooper. Solid information about handling a rope, roping dummies, and heading and heeling for practice and in competition. Also sound advice about rope horses, roping steers, gear, and horsemanship.

WELL-SHOD by Don Baskins
160 pages, 300 black-and-white photos and illustrations. A horse-shoeing guide for owners and farriers. The easy-to-read text, illustrations, and photos show step-by-step how to trim and shoe a horse for a variety of uses. Special attention is paid to corrective shoeing techniques for horses with various foot and leg problems.

WESTERN HORSEMANSHIP by Richard Shrake
144 pages and 150 photographs. Complete guide to riding western horses.

WESTERN TRAINING by Jack Brainard
With Peter Phinny. 136 pages. Stresses the foundation for western training.

WIN WITH BOB AVILA by Juli S. Thorson
This 128-page, hardbound, full-color book discusses traits that separate horse-world achievers from also-rans. World champion horseman Bob Avila shares his philosophies on succeeding as a competitor, breeder, and trainer.